OVERCOMING OVERTHINKING

 36 Ways To Tame Anxiety
for Work, School, and Life

Deborah Grayson Riegel, M.S.W. & Sophie Riegel

INDIE BOOKS
INTERNATIONAL

ISBN-13: 978-1-947480-82-7

Library of Congress Control Number: 2019916727

Designed by Joni McPherson, mcphersongraphics.com

INDIE BOOKS INTERNATIONAL, INC

2424 VISTA WAY, SUITE 316

OCEANSIDE, CA 92054

www.indiebooksintl.com

CONTENTS

DEDICATION

For Michael, Jake, and Nash, who have helped us overcome everything.

PREFACE

On June 6, 2015, the lead story of the Boston Globe's travel section was titled, "Preparing Kids for When a Parent Travels."[1] The article addressed the anxiety that parents and children feel when they're separated for trips that take at least one parent out of town. It also included practical strategies from parents and psychologists to address the stress, reduce the fear, and create a connection across the distance.

The accompanying image for this article was an above-the-fold, half-page, full-color drawing of a mom in a hotel room and a daughter in her home bedroom, both sleeping peacefully, with each one wearing one-half of a matching pair of socks.

That mom and daughter are us. For real.

We have used that single strategy—splitting a pair of socks—to help us deal with the stress of separations ranging from a few days to a few weeks. The writer included this technique and several others that we've used to overcome overthinking when we're apart from each other.

But being away from each other isn't the only time we worry. Not by a long shot.

Having both been diagnosed with anxiety disorders (three for mom Deborah, and four for daughter Sophie—we're always so competitive), we know that stewing, agonizing, and ruminating is in our DNA.

---

[1] Kari Bodnarchuk, "Preparing Kids for When a Parent Travels." *The Boston Globe*, BostonGlobe.com, June 6, 2015, https://www.bostonglobe.com/lifestyle/travel/2015/06/06/preparing-kids-for-when-parent-travels/ud1ZhHggFGhwvEZ54IUDUN/story.html.

When do we overthink? *When:*

SOPHIE

- Someone delays giving me an answer

- Someone's facial expressions don't match their tone of voice

- Something comes too easily

- Something good happens

- Someone stops texting after I see my message has been read

DEBORAH

- I am waiting for the doctor to call back

- Anyone says to me, "Let's talk"

- Either of my children get into a car

- My husband does something nice

- My husband does something not so nice (sorry, Michael)

...and dozens more.

DEBORAH

As an executive coach, keynote speaker, workshop leader, and author, I spend every day offering tips, tools, and techniques to help my clients manage the overthinking that tends to accompany big presentations, tricky conversations, and difficult conversations.

As a wife and mom, I am a thought partner in helping my husband and two children navigate the worries of daily life.

And in my personal life, I have been a world-class overthinker for more than forty years. It has only been in the last few years that I have figured out how to apply the mindsets, beliefs, and behaviors that I suggest to others for my own benefit.

SOPHIE

And as an author, speaker, and advocate, I've been all over the country to share my experience with anxiety to all different kinds of people, from parents to teenagers to educators to camp counselors.

After working tirelessly to improve myself and learn to cope with my anxiety, I find that it is my calling and duty to help other people learn how to talk about mental health, how to be resilient, ways to end the stigma surrounding mental illness, and so much more.

And while I'm not a professional (yet), my years of experience dealing with mental illnesses have offered me a unique perspective in sharing my strategies for overcoming overthinking with others.

As author Jonathan Safran Foer wrote in his book, *Extremely Loud and Incredibly Close*, "I think and think and think, I've thought myself out of happiness one million times, but never once into it."[2]

For those of you who think and think and think about the past, the present, and the future, this book will help you challenge your thinking, create new strategies, and connect with others so that you don't have to do this alone.

Because you're not alone.

We're right here with you. Starting now.

(And we're even happy to share our socks with you.)

Deborah Grayson Riegel and Sophie Riegel

---

[2] Jonathan Safran Foer, *Extremely Loud & Incredibly Close* (London: Penguin Books, 2018).

PART I

Why We Care About Overcoming Overthinking

DEBORAH'S STORY

"You're always waiting for the other shoe to drop."

Since as early as I can recall, this was how my mother described my perspective on life. And she was completely right.

I constantly lived in a state of hypervigilance, always watching and waiting for signs that something terrible was about to occur. When anything negative *did* happen (from not getting the best grade on a test in the class, to knowing that our family was having financial struggles, to my parents' divorce when I was in high school), I felt justified in my anxiety. See? I knew *something* would happen—and there it was.

Then I would feel a momentary sense of relief because the bad thing was over. And then, because the bad thing was over, my anxiety would start to build again, steeling me for the next setback or tragedy.

This was an exhausting cycle. And I'd never known any other way to live.

When I was a preteen, my parents sent me to speak with a therapist because I seemed angry and sullen. Or, more accurately, I *was* angry and sullen—and anxious. The therapist diagnosed me with generalized anxiety disorder, and we worked together for many years to help me manage my moods and my life.

Therapy made me feel supported and understood, but no less anxious.

As a teenager, my father recognized that my drive to be the best student in all of my classes was taking a physical and emotional toll on me. I was often up all night, overthinking in preparation for the next day's test or a term paper that was due, crying because I couldn't get it "perfect." (In retrospect, I was also crying because I was so tired.) He tried to help me put school in perspective, but I wasn't willing or able to hear it.

I developed a tic disorder (not diagnosed until I was an adult), where the constant twitching of my neck muscles led to repetitive-use cramps. My parents did the best they could and gave me a small dose of a muscle relaxer to help me on the days when I was in so much pain that I could barely hold my head up.

I was more anxious than ever. I couldn't silence my thinking. And when asked, "What are you anxious about?" I couldn't answer. I was anxious about nothing and everything, all at the same time.

In my college years, and into my adult years, I came to believe that living with the emotional and physical toll of anxiety was a given. My anxiety even justified it for me, reminding me, "If you didn't have this problem, you'd have something worse—so be grateful that this is all you have to deal with."

(This, of course, is not how life works, but my anxiety isn't logical.)

When I married my husband Michael, I realized that this way of overthinking—that something awful is about to happen—isn't universal. His outlook on life is, "I'll worry when there's something to worry about."

I found his perspective naive—and dangerous. "There's always something to worry about!" I told him. I realized that if he wasn't watching for a disaster, then I had to do double-duty and watch out for both of us.

This would have been OK (well, not *really* OK) if I had kept that to myself. But I found myself articulating every single worry to him every single time I thought of something to worry about. This meant that every day, when we put our kids on the school bus, I reminded him that we may never see them again. On every date night, I mentioned that we could suddenly get divorced. On every vacation, I brought up the fact that we could arrive home to a house that had been ransacked by robbers.

Every. Single. Time.

This was not helpful, or productive, or romantic, to say the least. And he told me so. So, I started keeping these thoughts to myself.

But I still had them every few seconds of every single day.

I started seeing a therapist who diagnosed me with obsessive-compulsive disorder (OCD). It was helpful to have a name to give my thought pattern and my need to talk about it. But therapy didn't help me manage these thoughts. And once again, I decided I would just have to live with them.

Then, Sophie was diagnosed with generalized anxiety and OCD. When I told her that I had those too, she was surprised and relieved to know that she wasn't alone. And while she got therapy and medicine to help her manage her disorder, I cheered her from the sidelines. I was so happy that she was getting the help she needed. I was proud of the work she was doing to live in peace with her mental illness.

And then, one day, my close friend Wendy and I were on the phone, discussing Sophie's positive progress, when she asked, "So, when are you going to get *your* anxiety handled?" I realized that she was having an intervention with me. I had long ago decided that I was going to live with anxiety, rather than try again to figure out how to manage it, and the question surprised me.

But I realized that I had a choice. Suffering was one option. Not suffering was another. And I was ready to try the latter. So, I made an appointment with Sophie's amazing psychiatrist, and three attempts at medication later, I noticed that I wasn't thinking about the worst possible things that could happen every minute of the day. In fact, I was *rarely* thinking about terrible things.

In fact, the most terrible thing that occurred to me was, "What if I am not *me* without worrying about the other shoe to drop all the time?"

And that's when I decided that, in my forties, I could be a new me: a me without the constant images of disaster playing on an endless loop in my head; a me without needing to talk about awful possibilities and play out every worst-case scenario; a me who worried about the things I *should* worry about, and who was able to consider and then postpone or dismiss the things that didn't need my anxious attention right now.

Both the old me and the new me are grateful for the mindsets, behaviors, strategies, people, and pharmaceuticals that have helped me get to this place—a place where my anxieties still show up, and then become helpful reminders of what's important to me.

I am no longer waiting for "the other shoe to drop." I am now excited to shop for new shoes, without worrying about how much they cost!

SOPHIE'S STORY

Before I tell you my story, you should know that if you want to hear the full version, feel free to read my first book, *Don't Tell Me To Relax: One Teen's Journey to Survive Anxiety (and How You Can, Too)*.

OK, let's begin.

Since I was a little kid, I have always felt anxious. Anxious about anything and everything. And that feeling started to consume me when I was in elementary and middle school.

In fifth grade, I suffered a traumatic bullying experience at a sleepover party that left me feeling more isolated than ever. And in sixth and seventh grades, I began to have obsessive thoughts about my family and my teachers. I also developed irrational fears of glitter, red markers, and germs. Soon, I was diagnosed with obsessive-compulsive disorder, as well as trichotillomania, which is a hair-pulling disorder.

When I diagnosed myself and came out to my mom about it, I found out that she actually had OCD and anxiety as well. Before I could really understand that this would be a huge support, I remember saying to her, "Well, your genes suck!"

She forgave me.

Going into high school, I started having panic attacks that left me physically paralyzed. Soon, I started medication, which worked for a while but ultimately stopped working, leaving me in even more distress. I was then diagnosed with generalized anxiety disorder and panic disorder. After trying a few medications, and even contemplating in-patient treament, I finally found comfort. This comfort came from the support I had from my family, the adoption of my rescue dog, Nash, and from publishing my first book and speaking all over the country to share my story.

Today, I am a member of Duke University's Class of 2023. I am also a two-time published author. And yes, I'm only a teenager.

I have anxiety. I have OCD. I have trichotillomania. And I have panic disorder. But none of that stops me. I'm lucky to be young and to have found one of my purposes in life: to help and educate people with anxiety and people who love someone with anxiety, and to inspire them to make a change in their lives.

OUR STORY
Why We Wrote This Book

DEBORAH TO SOPHIE

Why are we writing this book?

SOPHIE

Part of the reason is that there are so many strategies out there everyone seems to recommend or use that may not be helpful to everybody. The same advice is given to people with anxiety over and over again, and I think we have something new to share. Also, both of our experiences combined help us relate to people of all ages. But the biggest reason I wanted to write this book is that, when I speak, the questions I get are really fascinating, and I realized that in my first book, I left a lot unsaid. So, what better way to answer people's questions about my first book than with a second book?

SOPHIE TO DEBORAH

Why do *you* think we're writing this book?

DEBORAH

Not to be immodest, but when you are out there speaking about anxiety, many of the mindsets and strategies you share start with, "Something I learned from my mom is…". I realized that you had internalized a lot of my techniques and that these were worth sharing to help others who might benefit from this advice. Also, I have learned so much from watching you navigate your anxiety, and I wanted others to learn from you, too. Oh, to heck with modesty: You and I are smart cookies, and we have a lot of life wisdom to offer on this topic!

DEBORAH TO SOPHIE

What do you think parents should keep in mind if their kid has anxiety?

SOPHIE

The first thing that parents should keep in mind is that this isn't *their* fault—even if they passed the genes along like you did, mom. (Sorry, but I'm keeping it real.) Parents should also know that they should support their child in reaching out for help, and not to take it personally if the person they reach out to isn't them. And while anxiety isn't their fault, it is their responsibility to create the conditions that help their child feel supported, understood, and hopeful about the future. Finally, even though anxiety can feel like it's taking over their kid, it's only one part of their kid—it doesn't define who their kid is. Remind yourself of that—and remind your kid, too.

SOPHIE TO DEBORAH

What do you think a kid should know if their parent has anxiety?

DEBORAH

It's not your fault. It's not your fault. It's not your fault. (There. I've said it three times, which makes it true, right?) Even though an anxious parent might use language that feels blaming (which I hope, after reading this book, they will stop doing), it's often misguided and misdirected. And even if you're a typical preteen, tween, or teen—pushing the boundaries and wrestling for independence—you didn't cause this.

It's also not your job to fix your parent or to take care of your parent. That's what other adults are for—friends, family, and professionals.

What you can do is be compassionate, patient, and understanding, as well as be assertive in advocating for your own needs.

One tip: In my work as an executive coach, I often find my clients being especially hard on themselves, or reluctant to address an urgent issue affecting their lives. As soon as I ask, "What would you do differently if this were your child?" their approach softens immediately. They are much more likely to be caring and kind and take action.

What does this have to do with you? If you think your parent might benefit from help, ask them, "What would you do differently if this were happening to me?" And then encourage them to do just that.

Finally, living with a parent who has anxiety isn't easy. You're entitled to get the support you need to keep from getting sucked in. You can be caring without becoming a caregiver.

DEBORAH TO SOPHIE

Let's say you don't have anxiety, and your family members don't have it, either. Who else do you think could benefit from this book?

SOPHIE

You don't need to have chronic anxiety to be an overthinker. Most of us overthink at some point. It could be situational, like before a big test or an important presentation. And it can even be helpful at times if it makes you feel more confident, and that confidence positively impacts your outcome.

But how do you know when overthinking shifts from helpful to harmful? What should you do if "regular anxiety" starts impacting your happiness, productivity, and relationships? You don't need to have a disorder to benefit from the strategies in this book. Even if you don't think you are an overthinker, you probably know someone who is and may be able to help them. And, these strategies aren't just helpful for overthinking; they also provide helpful problem-solving techniques, interpersonal skills, ways to reduce stress, tools to make your life happier and more fulfilling, and so much more.

SOPHIE TO DEBORAH

You also felt really strongly about thirty-six tips, even though thirty-seven is your lucky number. Why thirty-six?

DEBORAH

I love the number thirty-six for our strategies because, in Judaism, eighteen (*chai*) means "life." Therefore, thirty-six (double *chai*) represents our two lives together, our two paths through anxiety, detailed in this book. We both hope that this book gives anyone struggling with anxiety a new and more hopeful approach to life.

DEBORAH TO SOPHIE

Anything you want to add?

SOPHIE

If our readers come up with more questions, I'll write another book!

Why Should *You* Care?

Chances are if you're reading this book, you already care. Maybe you care because you struggle with anxiety, and it's literally keeping you up at night. Or perhaps you care because you're noticing the signs in someone you know and love. No matter who or what the reason is, you care because you recognize that anxiety hurts, overwhelms, and paralyzes people. And the numbers reinforce what you already know in your gut.

According to research done by the Anxiety and Depression Association of America, anxiety disorders are the most prevalent mental illness in the United States, affecting 18.1 percent of adults and 25.1 percent of children ages 13-18; also, "Anxiety disorders are highly treatable, yet only 36.9 percent of those suffering receive treatment."[3]

While this book doesn't have a "treatment plan," it does provide many helpful strategies that you or anyone else can use to help manage anxiety, in addition to getting professional help. Reading this book—and sharing it with others—is a step in the right direction toward increasing the number of people who no longer need to suffer as much as they do.

This book probably won't be the only support that you or someone you care about will need. But it will likely be the least expensive, most fun, and easiest to share with others.

---

[3] Anxiety and Depression Association of America (ADAA), Facts and Statistics page. Accessed August 29, 2019. https://adaa.org/about-adaa/press-room/facts-statistics.

PART II

Challenge Your Thinking

Until you make the unconscious conscious, it will direct your life and you will call it fate.
— **Carl Jung**

SOPHIE'S STRATEGY 1

Treat Your Mental Health Like Your Physical Health

When I speak to groups, parents often ask me what to do if they are scared of giving their child medication for mental illnesses. And my answer is almost always the same: "What would you do if your child had cancer?"

They usually tell me that they would get their child access to the best medicine available.

"Then why should you treat your child's mental health any differently than how you would treat their physical health?"

This usually helps them to shift perspective and take the opportunity to examine their own beliefs about mental illness.

In our society, people tend to discuss physical problems all the time, from diabetes to broken bones to the flu. And when we have a physical injury or disability, our first reaction is to go to the doctor and get medication. When you wake up with a headache, I'll bet you don't spend days, weeks, or months wondering whether you should try to take medication for it.

So, why are we, as a society, so willing to take medication to ease our physical pain, but not our mental pain? This is a question I constantly ask myself, and what I've come up with is that we fear admitting we have "mental pain." But this fear, and this propensity to ignore when we are mentally unhealthy, is why mental illnesses are on the rise. If we learn to treat mental health just like physical health, we would be a lot healthier.

So, how do we do that?

Let me tell you what I've learned.

If you are feeling anxious, it's not particularly helpful to think to yourself, "Oh, it's just anxiety. There's nothing I can do about it."

Instead, ask yourself, "If my anxiety were a physical injury, what would I do?"

Chances are, your answer wouldn't be, "I would pretend that it wasn't an actual injury," or "I would be too embarrassed to tell anyone about it," or, "I would just ignore it. Untreated injuries usually just resolve themselves, right?"

No, you would not ignore it. You would probably wrap it in a bandage immediately, take some pain medicine, and schedule an appointment with the doctor or head to urgent care, depending on how bad the injury is.

Think about that for a moment.

You are willing to do all those things for your physical health, so you should do the same for your mental health.

If you're feeling anxious, do something healing for your mental health that makes you feel more supported, just like bandaging an injury (example: call a friend).

Do something to stop the pain (for example: take anti-anxiety medication or practice helpful self-talk).

Reach out to a professional and schedule a check-up (example: call a therapist or a psychiatrist). Usually, after taking these steps, you will feel a lot better.

We have been trained to ignore pain and distress when it is not physical. It is hard to remember that, just as we put bandages on a cut to stop the bleeding, we must do the same with our overthinking to stop our thoughts from consuming us. Even though it is hard, it is worth it.

DEBORAH'S STRATEGY 2
Learn Your Launch Sequence

I'm not sure if I'm an introverted extrovert or an extroverted introvert, but I am positive about this: Despite the fact that being a professional speaker looks a lot like I adore being around crowds and working the room, I would almost always prefer to be with my immediate family, with one or two close friends—or alone.

At the end of a long day of speaking, coaching, and consulting, I want nothing more than to get into my pajamas, order room service, and find an episode of *Chopped* on TV. I don't want to talk to anyone. I don't want to engage. I don't want to have to be "on."

Nevertheless, sometimes being social with others—even when it's not my preference—is part of the job. And for me to be present *and* pleasant, I need to recognize that connecting with others when I want to disconnect activates an anxiety launch sequence that requires my attention.

Here's what it looks like:

>**My need:** To be alone

>**My trigger (Any cue that prompts an increase in symptoms):** Feeling obligated to socialize

>**My launch sequence:** Tightness in my throat, scrambling thoughts to find a way out, feeling angry and sad. (Don't I sound like a fun dinner date?)

This sequence of events isn't a choice. It's automatic.

But what happens next is a choice.

Each of us chooses how we react to situations, states of mind, and people. Even though our responses feel automatic, when we can recognize our triggers, we can slow down our responses, consider our options, then choose what to say or do next.

How can we do that? By identifying what sets us off, recognizing what we can and can't control, communicating our expectations to others, taking responsibility for our reactions and responses, and planning for the future.

Here's how I handle my launch sequence:

1. **Name it to tame it** (see Strategy 15): "I am feeling anxious and sad because I would prefer to be alone to recharge and relax."

2. **Identify what's in my control:**

   ▶ I could say no to this dinner invitation.

   ▶ I am choosing not to say no because I would rather honor someone else's preference than mine.

   ▶ I can plan to take time for myself later tonight, or tomorrow morning, to recharge.

   ▶ Just because I say yes to this invitation, that doesn't mean I have to say yes to the next one.

3. **Identify what's not in my control:** The other person's reactions or responses to me saying yes or no to this invitation.

4. **Communicate expectations:** I can let the other person know that I probably won't stay for dessert since I need to get to sleep early. (Notice I said "probably," because if there's something on the menu that combines peanut butter and chocolate, I consider that restorative and therapeutic.)

5. **Take responsibility for my reactions and responses:** Once I have said yes to an invitation, I am all in. I will be pleasant, engaging, and engaged, and I will show up as my best self.

6. **Plan for the future:** Next time, I will let the person know in advance that I won't be able to meet for dinner, but would be happy to connect over breakfast or coffee the next day (time permitting) when I am refreshed.

OK, your turn! Below is a list of thirty-six common triggers (including many from Dr. John Gottman, professor emeritus of psychology at the University of Washington, and cofounder with his wife Julie of The Gottman Institute).[4] Find yours, and then plan to manage your launch sequence.

I get triggered when I feel:

1. A lack of affection	13. Impatient	25. Powerless
2. Blamed	14. Isolated	26. Rushed
3. Controlled	15. Judged	27. Scolded
4. Dependent	16. Like I can't be honest	28. Silenced
5. Disconnected	17. Like I can't speak up	29. Torn
6. Disrespected	18. Like something's unfair	30. Trapped
7. Distrusted	19. Like the bad guy	31. Uncared for
8. Excluded	20. Lonely	32. Underutilized
9. Forgotten	21. Manipulated	33. Unheard
10. Frustrated	22. Misunderstood	34. Uninformed
11. Ignored	23. Obligated	35. Unloved
12. Inauthentic	24. Overwhelmed	36. Unsafe

---

[4] The Gottman Institute, Gottman.com

SOPHIE'S STRATEGY 3

Name Multiple Perspectives

When my first book was published, I was invited to sit on a panel with a psychologist and a psychiatrist. We had an interesting discussion about what to do when kids label themselves "tough" to handle. I listened a while as these two professionals discussed this dilemma, saying things like, "I would ask them why they think they are tough," or "I would tell them to give themselves a new label and get rid of 'tough.'"

I had another perspective to share. What if, rather than analyzing the adjective or eliminating the label, we accepted it and added to it?

How would we do that?

Well, we would follow the first rule of improvisation: Never say no. Instead, say "Yes, and…"

When it was finally my time to speak, I said that I would tell kids that they are tough *and* smart *and* strong. I did not want to minimize kids' feelings by telling them that they need to choose a different way to describe themselves; I wanted to let them know that they have *many* characteristics—one of which may be interpreted as tough. This is how we name multiple perspectives, coexisting at once.

When I am anxious, I practice this way of thinking often. When I think, "I am so anxious," I ask myself, "Yes, and?" And then I think, "I am anxious *and* grateful *and* powerful *and* a little bit sad *and* excited for the future."

When I do this, I acknowledge my anxiety without making it the only thing I think about.

Another useful part of naming multiple perspectives when it comes to anxiety is learning how to distinguish *helpful* anxiety from *unhelpful* anxiety. An example of helpful anxiety would be feeling anxious the day before a big test, compelling you to study more. Unhelpful anxiety would be feeling panicked as the test is being given out when there is no time to study—and ruining your concentration. In the anxious moment, it is often difficult to make this distinction because almost all anxiety feels harmful. But learning how to recognize helpful anxiety, and learning to embrace it, is a way of naming a new perspective about anxiety: Anxiety sucks, *and* it is helping me right now.

So how do we figure out if our anxiety is beneficial or detrimental? We ask ourselves a few questions:

1. "If I didn't have anxiety right now, would my performance or attitude be more positive?" If so, the anxiety is probably not helpful.

2. "What effect is my anxiety having? Is it causing me to do something differently (study more or less for a test, prepare more or less for a job interview)? Is this effect positive?"

3. "Is there anything that my anxiety is trying to teach me or tell me?"

By asking ourselves these questions, it becomes much easier to identify advantageous anxiety.

Naming a new perspective is not easy. It requires you to have an open mind about your situation and to accept that your immediate reality is not the *only* reality. But if you can learn to name these new perspectives about your anxiety, you will be amazed at how free you feel.

Don't let yourself be trapped by a single point of view. Allow yourself to name something different about your anxiety—not instead of, but in addition to—and see where that takes you.

In the words of author F. Scott Fitzgerald, the "test of a first-rate intelligence is the ability to hold two opposed ideas in the mind at the same time, and still retain the ability to function."

DEBORAH'S STRATEGY 4
Challenge Your Catastrophic Thinking

In the Oscar-winning film, *Annie Hall*, Woody Allen's character, Alvy Singer, lamented: "I feel that life is divided into the horrible and the miserable. That's the two categories."

Hopefully, most of us realize that life can be divided into many other categories, including joyful and passionate and surprising and wondrous, along with, of course, the horrible and the miserable. What many of us don't realize is that we have the ability to anticipate the best possible outcome or the worst possible outcome.

Do any of these sound like you?

▶ You can instantly transform any ache or pain into a potentially life-ending illness.

▶ You can easily shift any scary news story into an imminent threat to you and your loved ones.

▶ You can magically mutate anyone else's workplace problems into sure signs that your job is on the brink of collapse.

When we let our minds wander down those back alleys into catastrophic thinking, you probably do one or both of the following:

▶ Overestimate unlikely probabilities

▶ Overestimate devastating consequences

So, what do we do? The experts say that catastrophic thinking needs to be challenged by more rational, logical thinking. Here are three ways to seize control of your brain before your brain seizes control of you.

1. **Name your catastrophic thinking for what it is and the impact it makes.** When your mind starts to wander down

those dark, what-if roads, say to yourself (out loud if it helps), "I am having catastrophic thoughts, and these don't serve me at all." Or, "I am making up a terrible story, and that's all it is—a story." Or "These thoughts make me feel horrible and I can change them." One of my favorite phrases comes from a magnet I saw on the wall of a yoga studio: "Don't believe everything you think."

2. **Remind yourself that even if the worst-case scenario should happen, you have the resources you need to deal with it.** Take a few minutes to list all of the inner resources you have available (your resilience, determination, sense of humor, and so on) as well as the external resources you have available (your family and friends, home, job) that you could lean into if and when you need to.

3. **Find the core of truth in your catastrophic thinking that needs real attention from you.** If you're constantly worrying that you're going to be fired, ask yourself what's actually going on at work that's raising your level of anxiety, and make a plan to address that.

Rather than invite catastrophic thinking, let's embody the words of Rabbi Nachman of Bratslav: "Thinking is more precious than all five senses." Let's shift our precious thinking from what we fear the most to what we believe we are truly capable of, in the best of times or—if the *worst possible scenario* should happen—in the worst of times.

SOPHIE'S STRATEGY 5
Ask Yourself A New Question

My mom is an executive coach. What this means is that she asks a lot of questions all the time, like "What's important to you about that?" or "What would success look like?"

I never understood how asking questions could be an actual job. I mean, I spend a lot of my time asking questions, from "What should I eat for breakfast?" to "When is the next test?" But after listening to my mom ask me questions, instead of getting frustrated with her, I realized what I had been missing. Coaches don't just ask questions; they ask the *right* questions.

I soon started to understand that one reason I felt anxious a lot of the time was because I asked myself the wrong questions.

Whenever we feel anxious, the first thing we often ask ourselves is "Why am I so anxious?"

There are three things wrong with this question:

1. A lot of the time, there is no answer to "Why am I feeling anxious?" A major misconception about anxiety is that you need a reason to be anxious, but this is not necessarily the case.

2. If you ask yourself this question and find the answer, you may become more anxious, which may start a spiral of anxiety. Because you are now consciously thinking about what is making you anxious, you are not focused on getting rid of the anxious feeling and moving to a healthier state of mind. So, you are now far more likely to continue feeling anxious than anything else.

3. The question starts with "why"—and questions that start with why tend to put people on the defensive. It makes you feel like you need to justify yourself—yes, even if you're the one asking the question to yourself.

So, if "Why am I feeling anxious?" is the wrong question to ask yourself, what is the right one? Well, I had this same question, so I turned to the person I knew would have the answer: my mom.

Of course, instead of answering the question, she asked "What do you think?" (she's such a coach!). But after a long conversation, we found out a good alternative: "How would I like to feel?"

Why does this question work?

1. There is an answer. And probably more than one.

2. This question gets you actively thinking about feeling better, which means that you are more likely to actually feel better.

3. It puts you in control of creating the future you want.

4. It doesn't ask why.

I knew my mom was brilliant, but I had to try it out for myself. The next time I felt anxious, I shoved "Why am I feeling anxious?" to the side and instead asked myself, "How would I like to feel?"

"I would like to feel calmer," I thought to myself.

"What can I do to feel that way?" I asked myself.

"I can go outside and take a walk. Or maybe I can watch a movie to distract myself." As soon as I had that answer, I went downstairs and watched *Finding Nemo*. And after doing that, I felt a lot calmer.

Let's break down what just happened:

I felt anxious and asked myself a helpful question. I answered my own question and asked myself a follow up question. I answered it and acted on my answer. I felt calmer.

The question "How would I like to feel?" led to action and this feeling.

This question is not the only right question, but it was a new and more helpful question. It was not a dead-end question. It did not make me focus on my anxiety. It didn't add judgement to my anxiety. And it allowed me to create a positive vision for my future.

Asking myself this new question was all I needed to do.

DEBORAH'S STRATEGY 6
Don't Create A Problem So You Can Create A Solution

Every time I come home from a business trip or vacation, there's one bag that never gets unpacked: my emergency supply kit. Unlike my regular toiletry bag filled with daily essentials such as contact lens solution, my toothbrush, and Chapstick, this is my "worst-case scenario" gear—for when the you-know-what figuratively, or literally, hits the fan.

I'm sure you can guess what's in there: medications for every imaginable digestion problem (and I'm sure you can imagine them), an antibiotic pack, antacids, nasal spray, cough medicine, bandages, alcohol wipes, topical cortisone cream. Short of packing a tourniquet in case of hemorrhage, I am very well prepared for a wide range of pain, pressure, and discomfort. I have anticipated a reasonable assortment of unpleasant possibilities, and while I have done my best to be proactive in preventing them, I am prepared to manage gastrointestinal, respiratory, or other physical setbacks if and when they occur.

The way I pack for a trip is a lot like how most of us, especially those of us with anxiety, pack for life: with strategies, tools, and techniques to anticipate all the things that could go wrong. We network because we foresee needing a new job one day rather than because it's a great way to buoy our knowledge, our field, and our relationships. We fall short of making meaningful philanthropic gifts to causes that support people during difficult times because we worry that we'll need that money for our own tough times one day. We avoid loving our partners truly, madly, and deeply in case they don't love us back with the same level of vigor—or worse.

Of course, life can and does disappoint us, scare us, and cause us both physical and emotional pain. But when we spend most of our time preparing for the worst, we let fear lead the dance. When we choose scarcity over abundance, we miss the opportunity to lay the foundation for what we will need when things *do* go our way.

Just because we're on the right track doesn't mean we don't have wants and needs. In fact, it's quite the opposite. When we're in a good place personally or professionally, it means that our wants and needs are being met more often than not, and there's no better time to reflect on what's working than while it's working.

The tough times will come. But don't wait for a problem to seek a solution. Don't anticipate a problem so you can plan a solution. And don't create a problem so you can create a solution.

Use the good times to reconnect with what you already have and to plan for what you want so that you can focus on packing less for life's pains and more for life's pleasures.

SOPHIE'S STRATEGY 7

Get Creative In How You Interact With Your Anxiety

There is plenty of great advice on how to solve conflicts with other people. But, often, there is little guidance as to how we can solve an internal problem, or something that is between our anxiety and ourselves. I'd been looking into this for a while and hadn't seen anything noteworthy, until my mom brought up Stephen B. Karpman's *Three Rules of Openness.*[5] These rules are designed for interpersonal conflicts (between people) as opposed to intrapersonal conflicts (within ourselves); however, they can easily be adapted.

Here are the three rules:

1. Bring it up.

2. Talk it up.

3. Wrap it up.

When we "bring it up," what we are doing is addressing that there is a concern or a problem. So, you can say to yourself, "There is something we need to address." You are saying this to your anxiety. And once you do that, you can start to "talk it up."

Ask yourself:

▶ "OK, what is the problem?"

▶ "How do I feel?"

▶ "What are you (anxiety) trying to teach me or tell me?"

▶ "How can we move forward from here so I can stop feeling _____ and start feeling _____?"

Once we are done talking it up, we can begin to "wrap it up." Karpman has many ways of wrapping it up, and I want to go over six of them and

[5] Karpman, Stephen B.. "Listening, Learning, and Accountability: Three Rules of Openness, Three Rules of Accountability, and the Adult Scales, Listening Scales, and Listener's Loops." (2012).

how we can resolve conflicts between you and your anxiety.

1. **Confession.** "Anxiety, you are making me feel horrible." Be honest with yourself. Be honest with your anxiety. Confessing your feelings may not resolve the conflict entirely, but you will feel a lot lighter and a sense of relief.

2. **Compromise.** "OK, anxiety, you can have ten minutes of my time. After that, you are going away." Just like with people, resolving a conflict with your anxiety is easier when both you and your anxiety get something you want.

3. **Concession.** "Anxiety, you win this time." Acknowledge that you feel defeated right now. Recognize that this is just "for now". And then move on.

4. **Consideration.** "Is there something that I should be worried about?" Consider anxiety's perspective. Maybe it is actually trying to help you. Maybe it is just trying to scare you. But either way, look at the situation from anxiety's point of view.

5. **Compliments.** "Thank you for trying to protect me." Give your anxiety a compliment. Although it seems a little bit odd, welcoming your anxiety may allow you to see the upside of your anxiety.

6. **Closure.** "I'm done letting you control my life. I'm moving on." Let your anxiety know that you mean business, and that you're going to take concrete steps to control it, rather than letting it control you.

It is important to get creative in resolving conflicts with you anxiety. Why? Because anxiety is used to you reacting the same way to it. It is used to you either trying to fight it or just giving up all together. It is not, however, used to being treated like a person.

Using the three rules (bring it up, talk it up, and wrap it up) along with the six Cs for how to wrap up a conflict, you can start to gain control over your anxiety.

DEBORAH'S STRATEGY 8

Recognize A "Mazel Tov Moment"

If someone offered you an all-expense paid trip to a beautiful European capital city (known for its croissants, chocolates, and cute cafes lining cobblestone streets) to do the work you love, with colleagues you respect, plus have some time for sightseeing and eating, what would you say?

If you were me, you might just say no.

Why, you may ask, would I say no to a trip to Paris? Because this opportunity to be the keynote speaker at one of my favorite industry conferences conflicted with Sophie's first scheduled weekend home from her first year of college. And despite my offer to move her "home" to Paris for that weekend, she wanted to be in her own bed, eating Kraft macaroni and cheese rather than *macaronis au fromage.*

And let me tell you, that should-I-stay-or-should-I-go dilemma made me feel incredibly anxious. And yet, I had to tell myself *Mazel Tov* (Yiddish for "good fortune") for having this problem in the first place.

I will let you in on a little secret about my special breed of anxiety: it doesn't usually rear its head as a result of me having too many terrible, horrible, no-good, very bad things happening at once. It usually shows up when what I am wrestling with is a direct outcome of me getting what I wanted—and worked hard to achieve.

Like what? Like a client offering to bring me to France (as a result of past positive feedback about my presentations) which competes with me spending time with my daughter (whom I hoped would go away to the college of her dreams). And that's when I take a step back and take a "Mazel Tov Moment"—acknowledging that the anxiety I am experiencing is as a result of something worth celebrating.

Of course, many of us experience anxiety around challenges and losses. But anxiety also crops up during opportunities and wins, like having a baby (or in my case, two babies) after years of infertility—and now worry, "How am I going to do this on no sleep?"

Or when we get the job of our dreams after months of searching—and now struggle with, "How do I manage people who have been here longer than I have?"

Or when we ace the big test after weeks of studying, and realize, "Now I've qualified to take multivariable calculus—can I hack it?"

When we hit a roadblock that shows up on the path between our "dream come true" and "now what?"—even a roadblock that leads to anxiety—it's still an opportunity for a "Mazel Tov Moment."

Let me be clear: The "Mazel Tov Moment" conversation is not a denial of reality. The struggles, stresses, and strains associated with finally realizing a major goal are as taxing as those that come along with the pursuit of the goal itself. It's about acknowledging the current pressure as real *and* resulting from something good.

As Henry Kissinger once said, "Each success only buys an admission ticket to a more difficult problem." The next time you experience a win, make sure not to let the changes or stresses that come with it turn your win into a loss.

(And for the record, I ended up saying "oui!")

SOPHIE'S STRATEGY 9

Avoid The Blame Game

According to Michael J. Formica in *Psychology Today*, "Self-blame is one of the most toxic forms of emotional abuse. It amplifies our perceived inadequacies, whether real or imagined, and paralyzes us before we can even begin to move forward."[6] Most of us are guilty of blaming ourselves, especially when whatever happened was completely out of our control.

But even knowing this, I still fall into this trap, just like many of us.

I remember just a few weeks ago, I was thinking about why my dog, Nash, got under the deck when I wasn't paying attention. The deck is completely closed off with fencing, so when I found her trapped under there, I was scared and confused. And instead of immediately trying to help her, I immediately thought "This is all my fault." I blamed myself for not paying enough attention to her. I blamed myself for not checking the fencing thoroughly.

And while I was blaming myself, there was a terrified dog trapped under the deck who needed my help. Because I chose self-blame over action, Nash was all alone under the deck and I wasn't helping her. A few minutes later, I got her out and comforted her, but blaming myself stopped me from acting quickly.

So why do we blame ourselves? Well, when there is no definite answer or reason why something happened, our go-to strategy is to make up a reason. And when we make up a reason, logic goes out the window. For example, when I was younger and struggling a lot with my obsessive thoughts, I used to believe the old saying: "Step on a crack, break your mother's back." One day, after stepping on a crack, I came home, and my mom wasn't feeling well. The first thing I did was blame myself.

---

[6] Michael J. Formica, "Self-Blame: The Ultimate Emotional Abuse," *Psychology Today* (Sussex Publishers, April 19, 2013), https://www.psychologytoday.com/us/blog/enlightened-living/201304/self-blame-the-ultimate-emotional-abuse.

Blaming yourself is the easy option, although it makes us all feel horrible. So, what can we do to stop the blame train from running?

Look at the situation from someone else's perspective.

Acknowledge your thoughts that are telling you that you caused the problem. Then ask yourself "What can I do *now* to help the situation?"

Act before you get a chance to get in your head.

The blame game is real. We all want answers, so blaming another person or ourselves somehow makes us feel fulfilled. But at the same time, with all the blame building up, we start to feel empty and heavy and sad.

It is hard to understand that when something happens, there doesn't need to be a reason. It doesn't need to be someone's fault.

We don't want to focus on the what-ifs or the I-should-have-dones.

Instead, we can focus on the future. We can think "How do we avoid similar mistakes?" Or, "What can I do now to make the situation better?"

And finally, we can think, "OK, this happened. Now let's move on."

DEBORAH'S STRATEGY 10

Detach From A Single Outcome

Picture this: you're sitting at the kitchen table with your family, enjoying a relaxing dinner, catching up on everyone's day, and the home phone rings. Despite your "no phones at dinner" rule (well, more of a guideline, really), you get up and check the caller ID. It's the alumni association of your college, or it's a hotel chain, or a local business that installs solar panels.

Do you answer the call?

If you're like me, probably not. Why not? Because it's dinner time (and there are *tater tots!*), and you don't want to be sold to.

That's not to say you don't ever want to buy something. But most of us don't like feeling the pressure of talking to someone who clearly has one outcome—and one outcome only—that they're committed to: getting a quick yes from us. (This mindset, and the aggressive behavior that it drives, comes at a cost. According to HubSpot research, only 17 percent of salespeople consider themselves "pushy," compared to 50 percent of prospects who see them that way.)

Guess what? We're all selling something—and we're often selling *ourselves* something that we are determined to buy now, as-is. Like what? Like selling ourselves on a new weight-loss plan ("This time it will work for sure"). Or an extracurricular activity ("The lead role in *Rent* will be mine"). Or a parenting solution ("With this new approach, tantrums stop *today*"). And when what we want doesn't turn out the way we want it (or even when we get the first inkling that it might not), we can start to feel anxious.

So, here's a mindset I learned in coaching school that has stuck with me: "The person who is most attached to a particular outcome has the most to lose."

In other words, if you are completely and deeply committed to a situation turning out one specific way—and that one way only—

you have a lot invested in a single result. What does this mean for you? It means that getting exactly what you want, when you want it, is one good outcome. But if it is the *only* way you're measuring success, you're going to experience a lot of failure, setbacks, and rejection. And yes, anxiety.

So, let's go back to salespeople for a second. While winning the sale right now may be one outcome that they're attached to, there are additional worthwhile outcomes to consider, like gaining some useful insight about the prospect that may help win a bigger sale down the road. Or getting a referral. Or even getting a yes from the prospect to the idea of reaching out again in a few months, when they have a better sense of budgets and priorities. While none of these are a "yes, I'll take 10,000 of whatever you're selling," they're all good outcomes.

Consider this:

- ▶ *Your new weight loss plan will work this time* is one possible good outcome.

- ▶ Another good outcome could be that you'll quickly discover what *won't* work for you over the long-term (like *green smoothies only*, or *no desserts ever*).

- ▶ Another one? You won't lose as much weight as you wanted, but you will have gained a lot of energy—energy you haven't felt in years.

- ▶ Still want more? You inspired your best friend/significant other/colleague to take better care of his or her health by setting a good example.

Finally, consider this: you can only spot another good outcome if you detach from the one outcome you're committed to.

SOPHIE'S STRATEGY 11

Accept That You Will Make Mistakes

We often define ourselves by our flaws. Maybe you procrastinated on a big project, and ended up turning in work that was subpar. Or perhaps you said yes to something when you really wanted to say no, and ended up suffering through the process. Or possibly you turned down an opportunity because you were scared—and missed a really big payoff.

The myth—the mistaken belief—is that as soon as we make a mistake, we *become* the mistake. And this myth drives us to avoid failure at all costs, and to always strive for perfection. However, there are many more negative consequences than advantages to this mindset.

Throughout middle school and into high school, I struggled to accept myself for who I was. I remember a competition in AP physics class to see who could make the highest free-standing structure using two pieces of paper, a strip of tape, and a paperclip. Not to anyone's surprise, my structure was over three feet high, and it was by far the highest in the class.

But I did not accept that success.

I focused on my initial mistake of not cutting the strip of tape in half, because if I had, I would have been able to attach my final strip of paper to the top of the structure. In my mind, I was a failure.

But what I failed to realize was that making mistakes is not only inevitable; it is necessary. We often learn far more from our mistakes than our successes, even though successes often feel better. Success brings short-term happiness, but learning from your failure brings a lifetime's worth of lessons.

So, what does this have to do with anxiety? Well, when we experience anxiety, oftentimes we try to be perfect.

For me, when I was struggling with managing my trichotillomania, I thought I was a failure for pulling out five hairs, even when, the day before, I had pulled twenty-five. I had improved, but I was still not perfect. And that is what I focused on. It was *all* I focused on. I could not accept that it was OK to make mistakes, to have setbacks, and to allow myself room for error. And that was why my anxiety skyrocketed.

Not only did I have anxiety from just my anxiety disorders; I was also anxious about making mistakes in my journey to deal with that anxiety. It was my stubbornness and my inability to acknowledge imperfect improvements *as successes* that led me to learn this lesson.

Tasha Eurich, author of *Insight: The Surprising Truth About How Others See Us, How We See Ourselves, and Why the Answers Matter More Than We Think*, wrote, "Where self-esteem means thinking you're amazing regardless of the objective reality, self-acceptance (also called self-compassion by some researchers) means *understanding our objective reality and choosing to like ourselves anyway*….Encouragingly, self-acceptance delivers all of the advertised benefits of self-esteem with few of the costs. Though the two are identical predictors of happiness and optimism, only people high in self-acceptance hold positive views of themselves that aren't dependent on external validation."[7]

Eurich made it very clear that accepting ourselves for who we are, including all of the mistakes we have made and will make, will help us feel a sense of internal validation, which will ultimately lead to a decrease in anxiety that results from wanting external approval.

So, how do we learn to accept that our battle with mental illness will include missing the mark? We start by asking ourselves this: "What do I value more? Perfection or satisfaction? Do I want to live my life trying to avoid mistakes, or can I accept that I will make mistakes, and ultimately feel more content with who I am?"

It is inevitable that you will make mistakes. It is often out of our control. But how you react to those mistakes, and whether you can accept them and move forward, is entirely in your control.

---

[7] Eurich, Tasha, *Insight: The Surprising Truth about How Others See Us, How We See Ourselves, and Why the Answers Matter More than We Think*. New York: Currency, 2018.

DEBORAH'S STRATEGY 12

Tell Yourself A New Story

After I have sent a proposal to a client, or left a message for a friend, or had blood drawn at the doctor, I have to wait patiently to hear back.

Guess what isn't my strong suit? Patience. (It might be more accurate to say it's my null set.)

I would rather do almost anything than wait without knowing what's coming next. Truth be told, I would often rather hear bad news than no news, because at least bad news is *something*. No news is *nothing*—nothing other than time and space for me to make up a story.

And those stories always make me feel anxious.

What kind of stories?

> ▶ A story about how the client I've sent a proposal to is deciding to hire someone else.

> ▶ A story about how my friend is mad at me for something I can't remember doing (but probably did).

> ▶ A story about how the doctor is trying to figure out how to tell me that I'm dying.

In other words, it's rarely a story with a happy ending. And I know I'm not alone.

According to neurologist Robert Burton, MD, author of *Where Science and Story Meet*, "because we are compelled to make stories, we are often compelled to take incomplete stories and run with them. With a half-story from science in our minds, we earn a dopamine "reward" every time it helps us understand something in our world—even if that explanation is incomplete or wrong."[8]

---

[8] Burton, Robert, "Where Science and Story Meet—Preview Issue: The Story of Nautilus." *Nautilus*, April 22, 2013. http://nautil.us/issue/0/the-story-of-nautilus/where-science-and-story-meet.

In other words, filling in the blanks makes us feel good, even if the story we're creating isn't a good one.

I've rarely experienced a situation in which I haven't heard from a friend or family member in a while and thought to myself, "I bet they haven't spoken to me in a while because they're planning my surprise party—and they don't want to slip!"

But what if I *did* start to think that? What if I realized that, since I am making up a story, I could just as easily make up one with a happy ending as one with a devastating outcome? What if I became less paranoid and more *pronoid*—believing that people are conspiring to make good things happen for me?

While I am still working on developing this as a regular habit, I can tell you the practice that I am consistent with: separating facts from interpretation, calling myself out on storytelling, and considering other possible stories.

Like what? Like this:

SCENARIO 1

Fact: I haven't heard back from my client yet on the proposal I sent.

Interpretation: The client is going with someone else.

Storytelling Call-Out: The story I'm *making up* is that I haven't heard back because the client is going with someone else. And that's all it is—a made-up story.

Other Possible Stories: The client is on vacation; the client needs to get approval from her manager to move ahead with me; the client had an urgent matter that took priority over getting back to me.

SCENARIO 2

Fact: My friend hasn't returned my call.

Interpretation: I did something to upset my friend.

Storytelling Call-Out: The story I'm *making up* is that my friend is angry with me, and doesn't want to call me back. That's possible—and it's unlikely.

Other Possible Stories: My friend has a work crisis that's taking up her time right now; my friend has so much going on that she wants to talk to me about that she's waiting to return her call until she has uninterrupted time; my friend just sent me a present today, and wants to wait to call me back until I get it.

SCENARIO 3

Fact: My doctor has not told me the results of my blood work.

Interpretation: I'm dying.

Storytelling Call-Out: The story I'm *making up* is that I'm dying and the doctor wants to figure out the best way to break the news to me. Yup, sounds exactly like the kind of tragic story I would concoct.

Other Possible Stories: The lab results aren't back yet; the doctor hasn't read my results yet; the doctor has read my results, and needs to call folks who have bad news before she calls people like me, who are getting good news.

So, the next time you find yourself making up a story that both makes you feel anxious because of the horrific possibilities *and* makes you feel better for having tried to make sense of the world, remember to call yourself on the fact that it's just a story. And if you're going to go through the effort of making something up, why not make up something that makes you smile?

I myself am made entirely of flaws,
stitched together with good intentions.
—**Augusten Burroughs**

PART III

Create New Strategies

If you don't want to burn out, stop living like you're on fire.
—**Brené Brown**

SOPHIE'S STRATEGY 13

Change Your Language

My mom always told me that "words create worlds," meaning that language shapes your reality. I never really "got it" until I was diagnosed with not one, but four different anxiety disorders: obsessive-compulsive disorder, trichotillomania, generalized anxiety disorder, and panic disorder.

That's a LOT of words. And those words rocked my world.

Most conversations about my anxiety have started and ended with the same words: "Relax. You have nothing to worry about." Honestly, I used to say these things to my friends all the time. But when I was diagnosed with mental illnesses, with something that would change my life forever, I started to understand how hurtful these statements are. These words deny someone's reality.

The idea that "words create worlds" led me to my goal, which is to reduce the stigma surrounding mental health by changing the way we talk about it. The way we talk to others who are dealing with anxiety and also to ourselves has a major impact on how we feel. Learning to say supportive things, as opposed to minimizing our own and others' feelings, is how we can cope with anxiety and mental illness.

Here are the things we often say to ourselves or to other people:

"Stop overreacting." Instead, say "This is hard and I am sorry you are dealing with this." What is nice about this is you can say it to yourself and to someone else who is struggling with anxiety.

"Why are you so needy?" Instead, ask, "Can you describe how you are feeling?" Or "Can you show me where you are feeling the most tension?" These questions are more supportive, but more importantly, they are grounding. When you ask someone to describe their feelings or physically point to where they are feeling anxious, it allows that person to distract themselves from their racing thoughts.

"Just breathe." Don't issue commands, either to yourself or to anyone else who may be dealing with anxiety. Instead, ask, "Can we breathe together?" or if you are talking to yourself, ask "Could taking some deep breaths be helpful?"

"You always get over this. You are fine." When people are anxious, rational thinking dissolves. So, yes, I do know that I get through it every time. But that's not what I need to hear at the moment. Try saying, "I'm sure this feels like it is never going to end. Let me know if there is anything I can do for you." Or let yourself know that, for a short amount of time, it is fine to feel like this isn't going to end.

"There is nothing to worry about." If you are talking to someone else, it is unsupportive to say this. Instead, say "This must be very stressful for you." If you are thinking this when you are dealing with anxiety, remember to be kind to yourself. Say to yourself, "I am feeling anxious. Let's think about why I might be feeling this way."

"You must be worried about something." Oftentimes, people assume that anxiety must be about something, but actually, a lot of the time it is about nothing at all. Many anxiety disorders come from a chemical imbalance in the brain. In fact, generalized anxiety disorder is exactly this: excessive worry that can happen without an immediate cause or trigger. Try asking, "Is there something, in particular, that is making you anxious? If not, that's OK."

"Relax." When someone tells me to relax, I immediately become frustrated. I would relax if I could. Try asking if there is anything you can do to help the person feel more relaxed instead of just issuing a command. If you are the person dealing with anxiety, don't tell yourself to relax. Instead, engage in helpful self-talk or try to ground yourself.

Why are our words important? Because they impact how we feel. Our words create our worlds, and we are all trying to live in a world that is calmer and happier.

DEBORAH'S STRATEGY 14

Use Appreciative Inquiry To Identify What's Worked In The Past

"If we see only the worst, it destroys our capacity to do something. If we remember those times and places—and there are so many—where people have behaved magnificently, this gives us the energy to act, and at least the possibility of sending this spinning top of a world in a different direction

—Howard Zinn

You have behaved magnificently.

Let me say that again.

You have behaved magnificently. Even when you've felt anxious, overwhelmed (or underwhelmed), strained, and/or doomed.

And chances are, you don't remember it. If you're like most people, you're likely to remember the times you curled up in a ball in your bed, crying, or when you yelled at your best friend, or when you snapped at your partner, or when you ignored the bills piling up, or when you turned in a project late because you just couldn't concentrate, or...or...or...

You can remember those times as if they happened yesterday, right? (And of course, they may actually have happened yesterday.)

Every day, we have the opportunity to choose our focus: Do we concentrate on what's distasteful, difficult, dreadful—or do we focus on what's working well, what's successful, or what we want more of?

Traditional methods of problem-solving focus on what's broken. I like to mix it up by focusing on what's working now and what's worked in the past using an approach called *appreciative inquiry*, developed by Dr. David Cooperrider at the Weatherhead School of Management at Case Western Reserve.

Think about the language: *Appreciate* means to value and to grow. *Inquiry* is the process of getting curious. Bottom line: appreciative inquiry is the process and practice of getting curious about what we value in order to grow it. It's the study of what works well.

In *Switch: How to Change Things When Change is Hard*, authors Chip and Dan Heath call this approach "focusing on the bright spots."[9]

While a full-blown, formally structured Appreciative Inquiry Summit can take hours, days, weeks, or months, you can run a micro-summit about your anxiety right now to help you identify what's worked in the past so you can borrow from your own successes in the future—or even today. This is also a great method to use to support someone else who is feeling anxious, to help them remember that they have experience surviving—or even thriving.

Here's the plan:

1. **Describe a time** when you felt anxious and you handled it in a way that made you feel positive, productive and/ or proud. The more specific, the better. Start by listing the mindsets (perspectives, beliefs, or ways of thinking) that you chose in this situation that felt particularly helpful.

2. **Example:** I had submitted a proposal to a Fortune 100 client to design, develop and deliver a year-long leadership development program, and I was waiting to hear whether I had been selected for this project. I was having trouble sleeping, struggling to stay focused during the day (constantly refreshing my email was pretty distracting), and kept playing out how disappointed I would feel if and when I didn't win the work.

[9] Heath, Chip, and Dan Heath. *Switch: How to Change Things When Change Is Hard.* Erscheinungsort nicht ermittelbar: Random House US, 2013.

That's when I realized that I needed to change my mindset:

From:	To:
I am going to lose this gig.	I may win this one.
I am going to feel awful when that happens.	If I don't win this one, there's always another one around the corner.
I'm not a big enough company to compete.	There's more than enough opportunity out there.
If I win it, can I even do it?	I'm going to learn something no matter what.

3. **List the behaviors** (things you did or didn't do, actions you took or didn't take) you engaged in that helped you successfully navigate this situation.

   ▶ I started reading a leadership book that would help me hit the ground running if I won the contract—and that would help me cope if I didn't.

   ▶ I looked in my database for existing clients who might want a similar program—and emailed them proactively.

   ▶ I exercised every morning to help reduce stress.

   ▶ I stopped checking email after 6:00 p.m. in my time zone.

4. **List the allies** with whom you engaged or relied on to help you successfully navigate this situation.

   ▶ My husband, Michael

   ▶ My coaches, Pamela and Ann

   ▶ My colleague, Thom

   ▶ Nash, my dog (who thinks she's a person, so it totally counts)

5. Name what you are *proudest of* regarding yourself in that situation.

    ▶ I didn't isolate myself, as I normally would.

    ▶ I truly believed that if it wasn't this project, another one would be right around the corner.

    ▶ I remembered to ask for help from colleagues, which I usually forget to do.

6. Record your answers somewhere so that you have a go-to list of helpful *mindsets*, *behaviors*, *allies*, and *sources of pride* that you can draw from the next time you're feeling anxious.

    ▶ I think I just published mine in a book.

As Albert Einstein put it, "The world we have created is a product of our thinking; it cannot be changed without changing our thinking."

SOPHIE'S STRATEGY 15

"Name It To Tame It"

Since I was able to talk, my mom asked me to name my feelings.

If I said that I didn't feel happy, she asked me to name my feelings more specifically, like saying that I was frustrated, or angry, or confused, etc.

Why did she have me do this? Because according to author and psychiatrist Dr. Daniel Siegel—and my mom—you need to "name it to tame it."

When I was in middle school, I walked around with this sinking feeling in my chest. It felt like any minute, the world was about to collapse on top of me. Now, at the time, I had no idea that this feeling wasn't "normal." But looking back, I know now that it was all part of my OCD and my anxiety.

If, back then, I had been able to name my feelings—overwhelmed and scared—I may have been better able to control them. I may have been able to learn my triggers. To admit that I needed help earlier.

But, as we all know, hindsight is 20/20, and there is no point in dwelling on past mistakes unless they help you with your future.

So how do we "name it to tame it"?

We can start by thinking about how we are feeling.

1. Ask yourself "How am I feeling?"

   ▶ Make sure you give the feeling a name, not a description. So, for example, say "I feel *nervous* about my upcoming job interview," instead of "I feel like my job interview won't go well." Once you've named the feeling (in this case, nervous or anxious), you can start to work with that. If you're having trouble, you can use the chart on the next few pages to help you name your feelings.

2. Ask yourself, "What is contributing to this feeling?" (If you can think of a specific trigger, that's great; when we can't identify the trigger, our minds tend to wander. And oftentimes, that leads to a spiral of anxiety.)

3. Use the steps from Strategy 5, in which you ask yourself a different question: "How would I like to feel?"

By following these steps and naming our feelings, we make them much less powerful. Once you know what you are feeling, you are the one in control. And when you are in control, your feelings don't control you.

The most important "name it to tame it" moment for me was when I was officially diagnosed with obsessive-compulsive disorder. For years before, I had had horrible thoughts in my head (obsessions) and I acted on them (compulsions). I didn't know that this was not something that everyone did, and what I was dealing with had a name.

But once I found out that there was, in fact, a name for what was going on with me, I immediately felt better. I no longer said to myself "What the hell is going on?"

I could now say "Sophie, this is just your OCD."

I named it, and I tamed it.

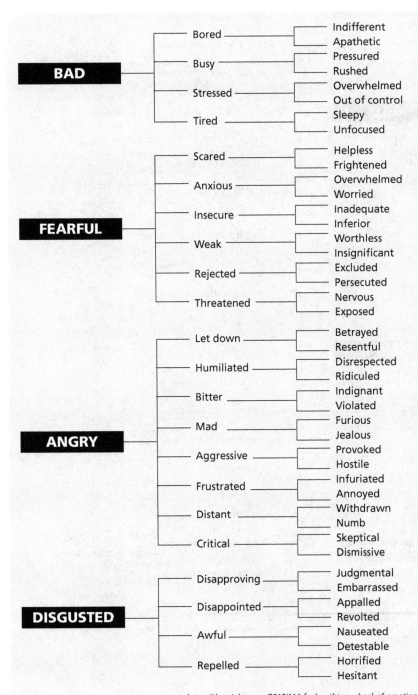

source: https://themighty.com/2018/11/i-feel-nothing-wheel-of-emotions/

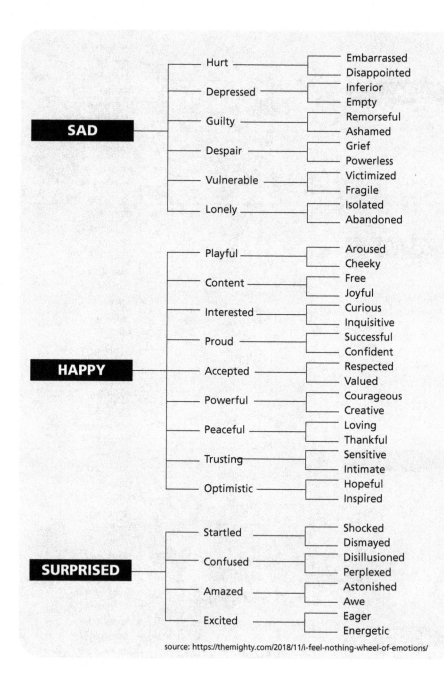

source: https://themighty.com/2018/11/i-feel-nothing-wheel-of-emotions/

DEBORAH'S STRATEGY 16

Remember To H.A.L.T.

A month after we first met, my future husband Michael and I took our first camping vacation near New Hope, PA. The flowers, the trees, and yes, the romance, were all in full bloom. We walked the quaint town's shop-lined streets, hiked some local mountains (fine, hills) and told one another our dreams for the future.

That is, until suddenly and without warning, I became uncommunicative.

Now, if you know me at all, you know that to get me to stop talking practically requires an act of congress or a roll of duct tape. But on this particular day, I just stopped. I was reduced to monosyllabic grunts in response to Michael's increasing concern about my growing silence. Had he said the wrong thing? No. Had I spotted a bear? No. Well, then, what was it?

I didn't know, and in fact, had no idea what had happened until we sat down at a local pub and I wolfed down two dinner rolls without coming up for air. Within minutes, I felt my life force reentering my body. I smiled sheepishly at Michael and announced, "I think I was just hungry."

As relieved as Michael was that this—my hunger—was the only problem in our relationship so far, he was also flummoxed. How could I not know? The answer was that I did know about twenty minutes before the shutdown occurred that I was feeling peckish, but over time, I just focused on feeling tense, edgy and annoyed. And by that time, I had ground to a complete communication halt.

Or, shall I say a complete H.A.L.T.: Hungry, Angry, Lonely, Tired.

These four emotions can catch you when you least expect them and cause a significant amount of anxiety in yourself and those around you. And if you're a busy person (whether you're putting out fires at work, managing the kids' homework at home, or just busy falling in love) chances are, you may ignore or delay the care and feeding of these emotions until you no longer remember why you've gotten crabby, short-tempered, or even teary.

That's problem number one.

Problem number two occurs when we engage in self-destructive behaviors that don't address the underlying core need, such as cuddling up with a pint of New York Super Fudge Chunk when we're actually lonely.

Problem number three adds insult to injury when we lash out at or withdraw from others, attributing our attitude to something someone else did when we simply haven't taken care of our own basic biological and emotional needs. The damage that occurs from constantly abrading ourselves and others because we haven't tended to ourselves can be off-putting at best and devastating at worst.

Why don't we address these four basic feelings: hunger, anger, loneliness, tiredness?

Here are five common reasons why, and what to do about them:

1. **There's "no time."** Sometimes we're simply too busy to deal with fulfilling our needs. Think about it: How many times have you told yourself that you'll grab a bite after you finish up the project on a tight deadline—and then forgot to eat? Probably more times than you'd care to remember. (And if you're reading this instead of having lunch, step back from this book and go eat something. I'll wait.) In this case, we need to remind ourselves about the negative impact of not dealing with our needs (like binging later if we don't eat when hungry), the positive outcome of dealing with our needs (like having more energy to complete the task), or both.

2. **It would be "rude."** It can seem impolite to get our needs met if doing so will encroach on others' needs or even on social norms. Hosting Shabbat dinner is often a challenge for me because I love to have people over (to

prevent loneliness, perhaps), but by Friday evening, I am exhausted. At a certain point, my fatigue reaches a critical point, but I fear that it is ill-mannered to change into my pink cherry pajamas while everyone helps themselves to a second slice of babka. So, I sometimes subjugate my needs in the interest of preventing an awkward situation.

What to do instead? I should deal with it directly and politely whenever possible. I'm sure nobody in my home would be offended if I said, "I hope this won't be seen as rude, but the Riegels are running out of steam. Can we wrap up some babka for you?"

3. **It's "unjustified."** Too often, when we feel these H.A.L.T. emotions arise, we don't feel validated to experience or express them. "How can I be angry at what goes on at work," my client Lou, a real estate developer, asked, "when 20 percent of our staff just got laid off?" Lou's perspective was that he hadn't earned the right to feel frustrated about the day-to-day stresses of work because he should feel lucky to have a job. But whether he should or shouldn't feel angry is irrelevant. He *did* feel angry—and trying to reason it away wasn't going to cut it. Stop trying to justify your emotions. You have every right to feel how you feel.

4. **We don't recognize that it's happening.** Hunger can feel like exhaustion. Anger gets masked as fear. Loneliness can be confused with anxiety. Tiredness can feel like sadness. When we don't have experience checking in with ourselves about what's really going on, we may not be able to name what we're feeling. Commit to noticing what your brain and body experience when you know for certain that you're hungry, angry, lonely or tired, and then commit those signs and signals to memory. (And as we discussed in Strategy 15, you need to "name it to tame it".)

5. **We don't know how to deal.** If you've never learned to effectively express your anger, or how to reach out when

feeling isolated, or how to eat the right amount when you're hungry, or how to decompress when you're tired, then you're less likely to deal with these emotions when they arise. Find yourself a friend, colleague, mentor, coach, or therapist who can help you develop healthy strategies to manage these emotions. They're going to show up again—so you'll want to learn how to deal when they do.

While our anxieties can be significant, deeply-rooted, and hard to manage, sometimes, all you need is a snack and a nap.

SOPHIE'S STRATEGY 17

Ground Yourself

I remember when I was younger, I would climb trees, dig holes in the dirt to look for worms, and run around in the grass barefoot. I used to have a much greater connection with the earth, helping me stay grounded and less anxious. But now, as a teenager, I find myself about to enter university life, I find myself keeping my shoes on, not digging holes, and being intimidated to climb a tree for fear of pulling a muscle.

I'm sure many adults feel the same way. In fact, a frequently repeated statistic tells us average Americans spend 93 percent of their time indoors.

Grounding, also called "Earthing," is a practice that a lot of people use to control their anxiety. The most common grounding technique I have heard, based on the work of Betty Erickson, follows these steps:[10]

1. Name five things you see (the TV, a tree, a piece of paper, a dog, a pair of scissors)

2. Name four things you feel (the chair I am sitting in, the socks on my feet, the breeze from the fan, my feet on the ground)

3. Name three things you hear (a dog barking, the washing machine running, the fridge buzzing)

4. Name two things you smell (my dog's feet, cleaning spray)

5. Name one thing you taste (the gum I am chewing)

By tapping into our five senses, we are able to feel more present in the moment and break out of the vicious cycle of anxiety.

Scott Jeffrey, founder of CEOsage, writes that "Being grounded can mean two things: Being fully present in your body and/or feeling connected to the earth. We've all experienced being grounded. We feel

---

[10] "About Betty Alice Erickson," Ericksonian Info. Accessed August 29, 2019. http://ericksonian.info/author/betty/.

"at home." But this is a fleeting experience."[11] So how can we learn to become more connected to the Earth? How can we practice grounding without feeling like it is a waste of our time—or too "woo-woo" to be taken seriously?

Here are five quick techniques to ground yourself in the moment:

▶ Eat something while paying close attention to the texture of the food and the taste. Eat without thinking about your next bite or your next meal.

▶ Look in the mirror and scrunch up your face. Look at which muscles look tense and when you relax your face, massage those muscles.

▶ Look around the room and count how many different colors you see.

▶ Move each muscle of your body, one at a time, starting from your toes and ending with your face.

▶ Lay on your back on the floor and close your eyes. Listen to the beat of your own heart.

If you do have a day or so when you aren't busy and you want more techniques to ground yourself, here are three more:

▶ Go for a hike and leave your phone in your backpack.

▶ Sit on the beach early in the morning or late at night when there are fewer people around. Feel the sand under your feet and take in all of the sights and smells and sounds.

▶ Write down (with a pen, not a computer) ten things for which you are grateful.

I know that it is often hard to find time or the energy to ground yourself. But grounding is a really important and useful technique in managing and reducing anxiety.

---

[11] Jeffrey, Scott, "9 Grounding Techniques to Reduce Anxiety and Center Yourself." Scott Jeffrey, August 14, 2019. https://scottjeffrey.com/grounding-techniques/.

DEBORAH'S STRATEGY 18

Make A Happy List And Choose Something From It

I keep a "Happy List" in the Notes app on my phone. It is my personally curated list of little things that give me a burst of joy, a modicum of calm, and a sense of satisfaction when I'm feeling anxious, overwhelmed, or sad.

I try to keep my standards simple: The items on my list are easily accessible most of the time (with a few items like "being outside when it's raining" beyond my control), usually affordable (although the longer I wander around HomeGoods, the more expensive it tends to become), and a mix of solo activities (yes, I prefer to shower alone) and those in which I spend time with others (and those others spend time willingly with me). It also makes me happy to add something to my list—or take something off if it's no longer bringing me good vibes.

When I'm feeling anxious, I pick something from this list of 36 activities and do it.

Consider making your list, putting it someplace you can find it without too much searching, and then—when you want it or need it—choosing something from it and seeing how doing it makes you feel.

Deborah's List

1. Reading magazines (*People*, *US Weekly*, *EW*, *Real Simple*, *Oprah*, and *Bon Appétit*, specifically)
2. Drinking a latte with a swirl on top
3. Going out for dinner and to the movies with Michael
4. Sitting on the couch with Michael early in the morning, just catching up and drinking coffee
5. Taking a hot shower
6. Burning a candle with a clean scent

7. Being in the middle of a great book (starting a new book triggers my anxiety)

8. Sitting in front of a fire in the fireplace

9. Finding a wonderful quotation that describes exactly how I'm feeling

10. **Smelling fresh flowers**

11. Having a new TV series downloaded on my iPad

12. Petting Nash, my (ok, our) rescue dog

13. Watching John Oliver with my son, Jacob

14. Going for a walk with Sophie

15. Hiking a tree-covered nature trail

16. Being outside when it's raining

17. Wrapping myself in a cozy blanket

18. Putting on fuzzy socks

19. Exploring any city

20. Trying a new restaurant

21. Trying a new and complicated dinner recipe

22. Baking something simple

23. Eating anything I've baked

24. Eating ice cream in my pajamas

25. Changing into my pajamas as soon as I get home

26. Getting a massage

27. Planning our next vacation

28. Going for coffee with a girlfriend in the middle of the week

29. Having company for Shabbat

30. Going out with another couple on Saturday night

31. Seeing what's up on Facebook

32. Watching *Chopped*—even if it's a rerun.

33. How I feel after working out (Note: Not the working out part. I do it for the afterglow.)

34. Walking around HomeGoods, mostly to check out what's new in throw pillows

35. Reading the weekend *New York Times* in this order: Travel, Arts & Leisure, Business, Metropolitan, Sunday Styles, Real Estate, Magazine section

36. Four Riegels (and Nash) squeezing into the big (but not big enough) bed to watch TV

Things that might make other people happy but aren't really my jam (but I'm including them here in case you need some ideas for yours):

▶ Talking on the phone (you've never seen anyone fake being asleep so fast as when our house phone rings after 7:00 p.m.)

▶ Shopping for clothes

▶ Going to the beach

▶ Going to parties or gatherings (unless it's at my house)

▶ Bars

▶ Concerts

▶ Organizing, unpacking, or cleaning up in any way

▶ Watching sports or attending sporting events (other than the Yankees during postseason or The Olympics)

▶ Physically exerting myself for any reason other than to burn off something I ate or am about to eat

▶ Thinking about decorating a room

▶ Getting dressed up

▶ Getting a manicure

What's on your Happy List?

SOPHIE'S STRATEGY 19

Write Yourself Letters/Notes And Mail Them To Yourself

One of the best experiences of my life so far has been backpacking through the Colorado Rockies at Camp Ramah in the Rockies for a week straight without showering. The not showering wasn't the best part (both for me and for the people I was traveling with); it was the freedom I felt being away from all distractions. I did these backpacking trips with about ten other kids my age for three summers in a row, and each year, we ended the trip with the same activity; we wrote letters to our future selves.

One year, I climbed a tree and wrote the letter. The next year, I sat on a rock in the middle of a river. The third year, I climbed up a rocky hill and wrote it as I watched the sunset. Then, these letters were collected and mailed to us a few months later, when school started to get stressful and when we may have forgotten that we had even done this activity.

Every year, I would get a letter in the mail. I always forgot that I had written the letter. And every time I opened it, I felt more secure. Like somehow, my past self was protecting me. Here is what one of my letters said:

Hi Sophie! It's me, Sophie! I know this is weird to get this letter but I'm telling you that you should listen to me. I know you better than anyone else. How is everything? Is your medication still working? Is school stressful? Are you feeling anxious about the future? I felt anxious about the future when I wrote this to you and now I know the future turned out just fine. But seriously, you need to take care of yourself. Don't say "I'll do it later," or "I have other stuff to do." Every time you say that, you are putting something else before yourself. You come first. Remember that.

After getting this final letter, I decided to keep writing letters to myself. I mail them to myself and when I get the letter, I wait a few months and then read it. This strategy has significantly helped me with my anxiety.

When I am anxious, it is hard for me to imagine that in the past, I was OK—that at some point, I didn't feel anxious, or that I did feel anxious, but I got through it.

When other people tell me that I have always gotten through my anxiety or panic, I don't believe them. But when I hear it from my past self, I believe it. I believe that my anxiety is temporary, and it helps me keep everything in perspective.

It costs less than a dollar to mail yourself a letter. It costs you absolutely nothing to sit down and write a letter to your future self. And it pays off quite a bit when you read the letter months later.

Why? Because we believe ourselves. We trust that we have our own best interests at heart. We have confidence in our own words and there is absolutely nothing more powerful than learning from your past to change your future.

DEBORAH'S STRATEGY 20

Pick A Different You From Your Portfolio Of Selves

In the social jungle of human existence, there is no feeling of being alive without a sense of identity.

—Psychologist Erik Erikson

On my good days, I feel fully, completely, and delightfully alive. I am grateful for all of the blessings in my life. I am proud of what I have accomplished. I am excited for whatever the future holds.

My identity on these days might be Supermom, or Entrepreneur Extraordinaire, or The Coaching Queen. (These identities don't make space for humility, as you may have noticed.)

On my rough days, I feel burdened by everything on my plate. I feel like I'm behind where I should be in life. I'm worried about what's ahead of me today, tomorrow, next month, next year.

My identity might be The Impostor, or She Who Can't Get Out of Her Own Way, or Deb of Doom. (I sound like I'd be a lot of fun at parties, right?)

But whether I am having the kind of day that makes me want to take on the world, or the kind of day that makes me want to get back in bed with my dog and my remote control, I do somehow manage to remember that I have lots of identities available to me. Furthermore, these identities don't require a passport or a wardrobe change. They simply require me to choose one to lean into.

In other words, I get to choose from my *Portfolio of Selves*.

What's that?

According to Blake Ashforth, a leading expert on identity at Arizona State University, in his book, *Role Transitions in Organizational Life: An Identity-based Perspective*, our sense of self is largely rooted in how other people perceive us. And for each "other" we engage with—a parent, a colleague, a boss, a friend, a child—we have a different "self" who shows up. As Ashforth writes, "A particular role calls forth a particular self such that the individual is actually a portfolio of selves."[12] This portfolio of selves allows us to be the person we need *at this particular moment* to feel better.

As author and Wharton professor Adam Grant shared in his podcast Work/Life, "one of the coping strategies is to think about yourself as having multiple identities. When people reject you, it helps to remember there's another you."[13]

And this strategy works even if you—in the face of your anxiety—are the person rejecting yourself right now.

So, on those days when I am feeling like "The Impostor" or "She Who Can't Get Out of Her Own Way" or "Deb of Doom", I flip through my Portfolio of Selves. These are the positive identities I know I have, based on how other people who love and value me experience me. When I can't trust me to see myself in a flattering light, here's who I choose instead:

---

[12] Ashforth, Blake E. *Role Transitions in Organizational Life: An Identity-Based Perspective*. New York, NY: Routledge, 2012.

[13] Grant, Adam, "WorkLife with Adam Grant: Bouncing Back from Rejection on Apple Podcasts." Apple Podcasts, April 16, 2019. https://podcasts.apple.com/us/podcast/bouncing-back-from-rejection/id1346314086?i=1000435037507.

WHO	WHO THEY SEE IN ME
Michael	Go-getter
Jacob	Loyal listener
Sophie	Compassionate confidante
My mom	An all-star
My aunt Laurie	Insightful niece and friend
My friend Wendy	Always available, for better and for worse
Nash	Loving mama who sneaks me steak

And this list is just a start. My portfolio includes my clients, my parents, my siblings, other friends, and even my readers (I hope).

Who would be in your Portfolio of Selves?

SOPHIE'S STRATEGY 21

Find A Mindless TV Show

People who know me know that from 8:00 to 10:00 p.m. Eastern on Monday nights, I am watching *The Bachelor*. I will not answer texts, calls, or emails at all during those two hours, because that is when I'm watching my mindless TV show. That is when I get to relax and distract myself from everything else that is making me anxious.

My mom and I share this ritual (even though she originally told me I couldn't watch something so mindless—and then ended up getting sucked in herself.) Even when she is away, we Facetime during the show and correct the contestants' grammar, discuss who we think is cute, and yell at the TV when the bachelor or bachelorette gives out a rose to the wrong person (#rightreasons).

These two hours are my favorite hours of the week. It's a time when everything else disappears.

When I tell people about my Monday night ritual, I frequently get teased. People ask me how someone so smart can watch such "trash." These people either have never watched the show before or they don't understand that this is a coping mechanism for me.

According to most people I talk to about watching *The Bachelor*, I am wasting my time.

But according to me, and my therapist, and my psychiatrist, and my mom, I am doing exactly what I need to do.

Whether you have an anxiety disorder or just experience occasional anxiety, it is important that you have an outlet. A happy place. Something you can do to distract yourself. For me and my mom, that's watching *The Bachelor*. For my brother, it's watching *NCIS*. For my dad, it's watching MSNBC (so, he's a little less mindless than that the rest of us, but someone has to maintain the dignity of our family's reputation).

To me, it feels so important to find a TV show that brings you comfort, joy, and calm. But what is more important than finding the show is setting a regular schedule to watch it. Don't just watch the show when you are anxious. Watch it every Thursday night at 9:00 p.m., or after work for a half-hour every day. Having this schedule helps keep your anxiety under control because you know *when* you are going to feel better. You know when you will have the opportunity to be distracted from your chaotic life. And when you know this, you feel like you have control over your life, which is something that anxiety likes to take away from us.

I'm not suggesting that you should watch *The Bachelor* (although I highly recommend it). I am offering you a way to stop your racing thoughts for a few hours. Becoming invested in something that I'm not directly involved in, that I cannot control, and that has no bearing on my life (like who gets the final rose), has been life-changing for me. Every week, I know that, with my mom beside me, I get to sit back, relax, and enjoy the show.

DEBORAH'S STRATEGY 22

Get Your Day Done, Fifteen Minutes At A Time

Despite the fact that I had wanted to be a mom from the time I was a little girl playing with dolls, I wasn't prepared to have two babies at once. I also wasn't prepared for the exhaustion of being awake, available, and on call, around the clock. And I never could have prepared for the depth of anxiety I felt being in charge of two little lives when I had never done anything like this before.

During the first month, Michael would get up with me for the 5:00 a.m. feeding and then head into work, since he was up anyway. By 8:00 a.m. every day, I would call him in the office and ask, "Are you on your way home yet?" And every single day, he would gently remind me that he needed to stay at work at least a few more hours, in order to not get fired, and to keep supporting our new (and explosive) diaper habit.

Once it became clear to me that I was on my own getting through the diapers, the feedings, the crying (mine included)—and the anxiety—all day, every day, I needed a new plan.

Here's what I came up with: "Just get through the next fifteen minutes."

Fifteen minutes felt survivable, manageable, victorious even.

And that's what I did. I planned my day in fifteen-minute increments. I willed myself to get through the next fifteen minutes, emotionally and physically. And I tried very hard not to think about the next fifteen minutes while I was in *this* fifteen minutes.

Guess what? I still use a fifteen-minute goal when I'm feeling overwhelmed, underenergized, or just plain *blah*. My babies are now grown, but I haven't outgrown this strategy.

Here are five things you can do in fifteen minutes:

1. **Tackle interruptions.** It takes more time and energy to stop what you're doing, deal with an interruption, and resume your original activity than it does to save up and address your interruptions in a single block of time. Schedule one or more fifteen-minute blocks during the day when you can tackle a chunk of tasks that emerged from earlier interruptions. And do your best to keep that interruption time uninterrupted.

2. **Decide what *not* to do.** If you've got a to-do list, chances are, there are activities on it that don't belong there. Maybe they're items you should delegate, or actions that aren't core to meeting your personal or work goals. Perhaps they're on that list because they've always been on your list, and now you're in the habit of keeping them there. In fifteen minutes of time when you're not trying to do something *on* that list, do something *about* that list.

3. **Blast through paperwork (or any other task you dread).** I hate paperwork the same way some people hate cilantro: with a burning hot passion. Nevertheless, I always have some stack of paper giving me the evil eye. So, I give it my attention in tolerable fifteen-minute blocks—no more, no less. And then I get a cookie.

4. **Change your scenery.** Even if you have no interest in heading outdoors into the elements, just stepping away from your desk for fifteen minutes is a great way to clear your head, connect with your colleagues, and maybe even get a new perspective on a challenge you've been working on. To quote the singer-songwriter Sheryl Crow, "A change would do you good."

5. **Acknowledge someone else's accomplishments.** It would probably take you only ten seconds to email a colleague with, "Great job on the sales pitch today. You nailed it!" in the subject line. So, imagine what you could do in fifteen minutes. You could pick up the phone and tell her so. You could walk over to her desk and tell her, while making eye contact. You could even send her that email and cc

a whole bunch of people who should know about your colleague's big win, too. You could do all of that, make her day, and still have ten minutes left to appreciate yet another person's special accomplishment.

(And if you're still looking for things to do in fifteen minutes, you can go online and send someone a copy of this book.)

SOPHIE'S STRATEGY 23

Exercise

I'm a five-time All-American racewalker. For the past few years, I have trained almost every day, and that is part of the reason why I have been able to fight against my anxiety and succeed. But in my senior year of high school, I took a break from racewalking.

My first book was about to come out, and I had been hired to speak in many places all over the country. I couldn't be on a book tour and train for races. I may not have changed too much physically from stopping my regular exercise routine, but I certainly changed mentally. I was tired more often, less motivated, and I was often sad. At first, I thought this was because my medication had stopped working again, but my parents offered a different perspective. They said it was because I had stopped exercising. And they were right.

Exercise is so important for both our physical and mental health. Research actually shows that exercise reduces the chances of developing chronic depression and anxiety. According to the National Alliance on Mental Illness (NAMI), "Like medicine in the treatment of mental illness, exercise can increase levels of serotonin, dopamine, and norepinephrine in the brain. It improves and normalizes neurotransmitter levels, which ultimately helps us feel mentally healthy. Other important benefits include enhanced mood and energy; reduced stress; deeper relaxation; improved mental clarity, learning, insight, memory and cognitive functioning; enhanced intuition, creativity, assertiveness and enthusiasm for life; and improved social health and relationships, higher self-esteem and increased spiritual connection."[14]

All of that information is great, but you know and I know that when we feel anxious or depressed, the last thing we want to do is go out and exercise. So how can we stay motivated to exercise when we are feeling crappy? Here are a few suggestions:

---

[14] Hibbert, Christina. "Exercise For Mental Health: 8 Keys To Get And Stay Moving." NAMI, May 23, 2016. https://www.nami.org/blogs/nami-blog/may-2016/exercise-for-mental-health-8-keys-to-get-and-stay.

Work out with a friend. Working out with someone keeps both of you accountable and motivated. And it gives you someone to talk to and interact with, so exercising is far less boring.

Pick a TV show that you can only watch when you exercise. For me, I used to only watch *Criminal Minds* when I worked out, so if I wanted to watch the next episode, I had to get off my butt and work out.

Vary your exercise routines. If you do the same thing every day, you are bound to get bored, so change it up.

Write down how you feel mentally before you work out and after. The only way you will believe that exercise makes you feel better is by listening to your past self.

Exercise is good for you. It's not just me saying this. Scientific research proves it. So, give it a go—now get up and go.

DEBORAH'S STRATEGY 24

Treat Yourself Compassionately

"I can't believe I'm feeling anxious again…for no good reason!"

"My heart is pounding and I'm sweating—when will I get a grip?"

"I always freak out. I'm such a wimp!"

Do any of these sound familiar? If you struggle with anxiety, chances are, you're also struggling with adding insult to injury: The injury is the anxiety, and the insult is being cruel to yourself about it. You probably wouldn't do this if your illness were physical.

"I have a stomach bug…I'm vomiting for no good reason!"

"My nose is stuffed and my throat hurts—when will I get a grip?"

"I always get urinary tract infections. I'm such a wimp!"

Sounds ridiculous, right?

Struggles with mental illness are no less worthy of a compassionate approach than struggles with physical illness. And considering how much our mental health impacts our physical health, I contend that we should give ourselves even more compassion.

Physician-scientists Stephen Trzeciak and Anthony Mazzarelli, authors of *Compassionomics: The Revolutionary Scientific Evidence That Caring Makes a Difference*, explain compassion this way:

"Compassion is an emotional response to another's pain or suffering involving a desire to help. Compassion is often confused with a closely related term, empathy. While empathy is feeling and understanding another's emotions, compassion also involves taking action."[15]

---

[15] Trzeciak, Stephen, and Anthony Mazzarelli. *Compassionomics: the Revolutionary Scientific Evidence That Caring Makes a Difference*. Pensacola: Studer Group, 2019.

While compassionate acts can and should come from others, they can and should also come from yourself. You are more likely to invite compassion from others when you are caring and kind to yourself. And the inverse is also true: If you reject compassion from yourself, you're likely to reject it from others as well.

According to Kristin Neff, Associate Professor of Human Development and Culture at the University of Texas, Austin, self-compassion involves three components:[16]

1. being kind and caring toward yourself rather than harshly self-critical;

2. framing imperfection in terms of the shared human experience; and

3. seeing things clearly without ignoring or exaggerating problems.

Showing yourself care and kindness doesn't just feel good; It can literally put you on a path to wellness. Studies show that when doctors are compassionate, their patients heal better and faster. And as a result of patients recovering more quickly and with fewer complications, physicians are happier and experience less burnout.

When you show yourself compassion, you are both doctor and patient, and you reap both sets of rewards.

People who demonstrate self-compassion feel more socially connected, have greater emotional intelligence, feel happier, hold a greater sense of self-worth, experience healthier relationships, and have higher levels of life satisfaction. They also experience less fear of failure, depression, shame—and yes, anxiety.

Here are ten ways to show yourself compassion in the face of anxiety:

1. Recognize that what you're experiencing is real and that it hurts, and that it's not forever.

---

[16] Neff, Kristin, "Self-Compassion: An Alternative Conceptualization of a HealthyAttitudeToward Oneself." Psychology Press/Taylor & Francis Group, 2003.

2. Give yourself credit for positive changes you're making.

3. Make only micro-asks of yourself, like "get out of your sweaty pajamas, take a shower and put on clean pajamas."

4. Pick something from your "happy list" (see Strategy 18) and do it.

5. Talk to a professional and take medication—without judging yourself.

6. Don't look at yourself in the mirror if you are worried about your appearance right now.

7. Eat your meals on nice dishes rather than take-out containers.

8. Remind yourself of your Portfolio of Selves (Strategy 20).

9. Post sticky notes around your house to remind you that you are worthy of compassion.

10. Forgive yourself for being imperfect—just like everyone else.

In the immortal words of Plato, "Be kind, for everyone you meet is fighting a hard battle." And that includes being kind to yourself as well.

Before we had Xanax, we had mashed potatoes.
—**Stephen Colbert**

PART IV

Connect With Others

Somebody in your life has to love you enough not to let you quit on a bad day.
—Angela Duckworth, *Grit*

SOPHIE'S STRATEGY 25
Come Clean (Tell Someone About Your Mental Health)

When I was twelve years old, I made the mistake of asking Google to diagnose me.

I let Google tell me that not only did I have OCD, but I was likely to commit suicide. This scared the crap out of me. I didn't want to have a mental illness, and I certainly didn't want to die. All of the anxiety that I felt about the Google diagnosis built up, and a few months later, after refusing to tell my parents or a therapist, I broke down. I was terrified of being judged or viewed as someone dangerous. I didn't know as a twelve-year-old that the only way to feel any sense of relief was to let a therapist diagnose me instead of Google, and to come clean about feeling anxious.

I know the feeling of so desperately wanting to tell someone that you are having a hard time, but also having your brain not allow your mouth to get the words out. It's an internal conflict unlike any other. A lot of people not only feel scared to come clean, but they also think that it either makes them weak for admitting they are having a hard time, or they think that they can handle it on their own.

I have struggled with all of these mindsets. So how can we get the words out and come clean when it feels like the scariest thing ever?

We start with baby steps.

First, admit to yourself that you have a problem. This isn't just a step in a twelve-step addiction program; it's a step when dealing with any struggle.

Once you admit you have a problem to yourself, you can begin to admit it to someone else. But who that someone is requires careful consideration.

According to the National Alliance on Mental Illness (NAMI), not everyone is able to offer emotional support—even if they really want to.[17] It's a skill, and some people have cultivated it, while others

---

[17] "Disclosing to Others," NAMI, Accessed August 29, 2019. https://www.nami.org/find-support/living-with-a-mental-health-condition/disclosing-to-others.

haven't. Being emotionally supportive can show up as listening well, demonstrating understanding, not judging you, only offering advice if and when asked, and even knowing when to give you a hug.

It's also important to keep in mind that someone can love you even if they can't support you in a way that feels helpful to you.

NAMI suggests that you make a list of the people you feel closest to *and* a list of the people who are emotionally skilled. Where there's overlap, start there. And finding even one person who cares about you and can support you is enough.

In my case, I was lucky. My mom is the person I felt closest to, *and* she is emotionally skilled (both professionally and personally). So I started with her—and even though I knew that she would love and support me unconditionally, I was still nervous.

Coming clean is a big deal. And if you don't feel comfortable actually saying the words "I am struggling with _____," you can write it down and have the other person read it.

If you decide to tell someone, it's hard to know exactly what to say. So, here are some steps you can follow:

1. You tell the person that you have to talk to them about something important. Don't make it seem like it is life or death (unless it is), but don't minimize the topic either.

2. Tell the person why you want to talk to them. "I want to talk to you about something that has been bothering me/something that I'm struggling with/etc." Then tell the person why you chose to specifically confide in them. "I am telling you this because I trust you and because I know you won't judge me."

3. Give some background. Say something like "For the past (time period), I have been feeling (describe your situation) and I am concerned about it." Give details if you want to.

4. Wait for a reaction or questions.

When is the right time to come clean? The National Alliance on Mental Illness said that there are three good times to do it:[18]

1. When you are well

2. When it serves a purpose or you need to explain a situation

3. When you are ready

I know that starting the conversation about mental health is hard, but following these steps will make it a little bit easier to essentially "come out" about having a mental illness or struggling with your mental health. And doing this will not only make you feel less lonely, it will also give you a major sense of relief.

---

[18] Ibid.

DEBORAH'S STRATEGY 26

When Asking For Help, Make Sure You Specify The Kind Of Help You Are Looking For

Psychologist Abraham Maslow once famously remarked: "When all you have is a hammer, everything looks like a nail." That's known as *The Law of the Instrument*—and many of us have one or two well-worn instruments, tools, and approaches that we use to help our colleagues, friends and families solve problems.

I know this firsthand: A decade ago, after I graduated from coaching school, I realized that my version of *The Law of the Instrument* was, "When you are a coach, every problem looks coachable."

Since one of the most useful tools in the coaching tool kit is curiosity, I asked a *lot* of questions. It got to the point that I would ask my kids, "How was your day at school?" or "What would you like for dinner?" and would hear, in response, *"Stop coaching me!"* (Fine. I don't care about your day, and you can make your own dinner!)

But seriously, the point was well-taken. Even though Albert Einstein himself said, "The important thing is not to stop questioning," the people around me said, "Please give your questioning a rest."

As someone who struggles with anxiety, I have found that people want to help me—and they are often limited by what they consider "help." Notice I didn't say that they are limited in their *willingness* or *abilities* to help—but they might only have a few go-to strategies that they initially think of.

So, I might need empathy on Monday, but my friend offers cheerleading. Or on Thursday, I need a brainstorming buddy, and my friend offers cheerleading. And two weeks later, I might benefit from someone playing Devil's Advocate with me, and my friend offers—you guessed it—cheerleading.

In my role as an executive coach, I now have a wide range of instruments that I can use to be helpful, depending on whether someone wants direction, advice, support, empathy, instruction, problem-solving, or yes, coaching. And it took a lot of work to cultivate a tool kit from which I could feel equally comfortable pulling out any instrument and using it well.

But the most important development for me was not assuming that I knew what help my client, colleague, friend, partner, spouse, or kid wanted or needed, but offering them a robust list of helpful approaches from which they could choose.

And when I need support for my anxiety, I know that I need to be specific in asking for the kind of help that would feel most helpful to me right now—and reaching out to someone who I can count on to do just that. While some folks have range (my Aunt Laurie is brilliant at empathizing, advocating, cheerleading, crying *with* me or *for* me—and basically anything else I need for support), others may only have one tool they choose to use. So, I'll call my brainstorming buddy when I need that, but I'll call a different friend when I need someone to just tell me what to do.

Here are a few instruments you can ask for when you're feeling anxious—and offer when you're helping someone else:

"What I need right now is for you to..."

- ▶ Listen without judgment
- ▶ Ask open-ended questions
- ▶ Play "Devil's Advocate"
- ▶ Brainstorm some new ideas with me
- ▶ Empathize
- ▶ Connect me to a professional
- ▶ Teach me how to do something I can't do on my own
- ▶ Share your own experience with something like this
- ▶ Make a pro/con list with me

- ► Give me a pep talk/cheerlead
- ► Help me prioritize
- ► Take notes while I verbalize my thoughts
- ► Help me develop some evaluation criteria
- ► Just sit with me
- ► Give me a hug
- ► Tell me jokes/show me funny videos/make me smile
- ► Assist me in making a plan
- ► Help me put this into perspective
- ► Remind me of the strengths and assets you know I have
- ► (And if I may be so bold) Share a really helpful book with me

SOPHIE'S STRATEGY 27

Ask Others To "Meet You Before They Move You"

When I was in seventh grade, every day I worried that someone I loved was about to die. I went to one of my teachers for help and this is how the conversation went:

Me: "I'm feeling really anxious all the time. And I keep having thoughts about my mom and dad dying. I don't know what to do."

Teacher: "Have you tried talking to your parents about it? Or maybe you should talk to a therapist?"

Me: "None of that is helping."

Teacher: "I'm not sure what to tell you. I don't know how to help you, sorry. Maybe you could talk to the school psychologist."

Me: "That's a good idea. I will do that."

When I left the conversation, I did not feel better. In fact, I felt a lot worse. Even though my teacher gave me decent advice, I didn't feel like she was supporting me. Looking back at that conversation now, I know exactly why; she tried to get me to do something without meeting me where I was.

The biggest problem people have when trying to help someone with a problem is that they are too quick to give them advice.

Here's how most conversations go:

> **Anxious Person:** "I'm having a problem with _____."
>
> **Listener:** "Why don't you try doing _____?"
>
> **Anxious Person:** "I've already done that."
>
> **Listener:** "Maybe you could _____."
>
> **Anxious Person:** "I don't think I can. This sucks."

Listener: "Go talk to _____ about it."

Most conversations involve someone with a problem and someone trying to offer an immediate solution. And why do most of these solutions fail to resonate? Or why does it feel like even if we give the best advice, the person isn't listening? It's because we tried to move them to a solution before we met them where they are right now.

So, how should these conversations go to meet the person where they are? Instead of telling someone what to do, acknowledge how hard the situation is in the moment for that person.

Why do we do this? We do this so that the person trusts us and is willing to listen later when we want to help move them to action. No one wants to listen to someone who has no empathy and who doesn't understand the problem.

Here's how the conversation could go:

Anxious Person: "I'm having a problem with _____."

Listener: "That must feel really confusing/scary/etc. How else are you feeling about it?"

Anxious Person: "I'm just nervous/scared/_____ that _____."

Listener: "I'm sorry you are dealing with this."

What happened here is that the listener didn't try to help the anxious person by specifying what to do. Instead, the listener recognized how difficult the anxious person's problem was and made the anxious person feel understood.

Now the listener can give the anxious person advice (assuming advice is wanted, as opposed to just having someone listen).

Before your next conversation with someone about a problem, remember to meet them before you move them. And if you are the one with the problem, tell the person you are talking to about this piece of advice, so your listener can better help you.

DEBORAH'S STRATEGY 28
Ask For Someone's Complete Attention

One of my favorite rituals when my twins were babies was to give them their nightly bath. I loved the one-on-one (-on-one) time with them, playing and splashing and just being together. Over time, they advanced from baths to showers, and from needing my help to wanting complete privacy, thank you very much.

But one bath-time ritual that Sophie didn't seem to outgrow during her tween years was keeping me company in the bathroom when I took a shower. Each evening after work, I would hop in the shower and pull the curtain closed, and then hear Sophie sneak into the bathroom, close the lid of the toilet, sit down and say, "So let's talk."

I was torn: I missed the privacy of being alone with my thoughts and my loofah, and I also appreciated the opportunity to have some deep conversations with my growing girl. But one day, my curiosity got the best of me and I asked her,

"Sophie, why do you always want to talk to me when I'm in the shower?"

Her answer caught me (literally) with my pants down:

"Because it's the only time I know you won't check your phone while you're talking to me. It's the only time I have your complete attention."

There was no shower long enough to wash off the sting of that pointed and painful observation.

And while I didn't know then that Sophie was having anxiety about not having enough time with me, I did know that she wasn't at all anxious about telling me the truth (and, for the record, she still isn't).

Ever since then, I've started paying a lot more attention to paying attention. I realized that I did so consistently with my clients (who pay for my complete attention), but I didn't do it consistently for my family, who are, in fact, the reason that I even have clients. And it's still hard—every day. There are a million things competing for my attention, between emails, calls, dinner, errands, expected and unexpected interruptions. But I am well aware that because of how hard it is to give someone your complete attention these days, it is a more precious gift to give and to receive than ever before.

In *The New York Times*, Sherry Turkle cites the costs of dividing your attention with people you care about include empathy, connection, and trust.[19] When you're feeling anxious, you know what you need more than anything else? Chances are, it's empathy, connection, and trust.

And while technology is surely a factor, another factor is our willingness to settle for less than someone's complete and undivided attention. We need to learn to ask for what we need from others in our personal and workplace relationships to feel heard, connected and respected, and we need to stop making excuses for ourselves for why it's OK to not be fully present for another human being with real and immediate needs and challenges.

Whether you're the one needing someone's complete attention, or you recognize that someone in your life would benefit from you, undistracted, here are ten things to request or offer to do:

- ▶ Close the door.

- ▶ Turn off all electronic distractions.

- ▶ Put your cell phone completely outside of your line of sight.

- ▶ Let other people know that you're going to be occupied, and for how long.

- ▶ Put a "Do Not Disturb" sign up and honor it.

---

[19] Turkle, Sherry, "Stop Googling. Let's Talk." The New York Times, September 26, 2015. https://www.nytimes.com/2015/09/27/opinion/sunday/stop-googling-lets-talk.html.

- ▶ Create a time buffer before your conversation so you can clear your head from your previous work or interaction.

- ▶ Make a list of what you need to do after this conversation so that you can be fully present, now.

- ▶ Notice when distracting thoughts come into your head, and then send them away without judgment.

- ▶ Let the other person know if something is interfering with your ability to be fully present, and then do your best anyway.

- ▶ Tell the other person, "You have my complete attention."

How do I know these techniques work?

Because I use them with my clients, my friends, and my family, and they thank me for not just being there for them, but for really, fully being there for them. And I also know these strategies work because I now, blissfully, shower alone.

SOPHIE'S STRATEGY 29

Find A Sit-in-the-Shit Friend And A Pull-Me-Out-Of-The-Poop Friend

When we talk about the importance of having someone "meet you before they move you," we are talking about two things: the meeting and the moving (see Strategy 27). While it is ideal to have a friend who can do both, it is rare to find the same qualities in one person.

So, what can we do instead? You can find one friend for each purpose.

The friend who will meet you is called the *sit-in-the-shit* friend. Why? Because this friend is going to let you talk about how much your situation sucks without trying to give you advice. Imagine you are literally sitting in a pile of shit. Someone comes along and from afar, says, "This stinks!" Now, that's not helpful at all for so many reasons, but the main reason is because this person doesn't truly know how much it stinks from where you're sitting. (Note: I am using "sit in the shit" figuratively!)

But, if the person is sitting in the pile of shit with you and *then* they say "This stinks," you might be more willing to listen afterwards, because they have experienced the same thing that you have.

When I tell you to find a *sit-in-the-shit* friend, I don't necessarily mean find someone who is also dealing with the same problem. I really mean that you should find someone who can empathize with you and let you know that they are willing to acknowledge how horrible the situation is—without trying to get you out of the pile of shit, at least at that moment.

Things a *sit-in-the-shit* friend might say include:

- ▶ Wow, this sucks.

- ▶ Oh man, this is a tough problem.

- ▶ You must feel horrible.

- ▶ This has to be hard for you.

Why do we need a *sit-in-the-shit* friend? Well, it's because they listen. They let you vent and complain without judging and without trying to fix your problem. We are often so quick to try to fix that we forget to comfort.

Now that you feel comforted and understood, you are ready to call your *pull-me-out-of-the-poop* friend. This is the person who may coach you to come up with solutions, or offer you some resources, or help you think about your situation differently.

Things a pull-me-out-of-the-poop friend might say include:

- ▶ It's time to think about how to get this handled.

- ▶ What have you tried?

- ▶ What do you want to do about this?

- ▶ I have an idea if you're open to it.

Why do we need a pull-me-out-of-the-poop friend? We need someone to motivate and encourage us to actually fix the problem, after we are done sulking about it (which is a very important part). It is often hard to start the process of trying to handle a problem, but a friend nearby who will guide you and give you advice makes it a lot easier.

So here is your task: Find one of each. Find someone to comfort you and find someone to give you the extra push you need.

DEBORAH'S STRATEGY 30

Get Up And Go Out Even When You Don't Want To

Despite the fact that I have my good days and my bad days, on most days you'll find me upbeat, cheerful, and energetic. But on my really bad days, I am like a totally different person. As soon as I feel that telltale blockage in my throat that signals the start of an anxiety attack, I go into super self-care mode.

Assuming I am at home, I put on my comfiest pajamas, lie down in bed with some favorite magazines, put on a recorded episode of *The Late Show with Stephen Colbert*, and just breathe. I try to get ahead of the anxiety before my neck tic kicks in, which will then add physical pain to emotional pain. And sometimes I cry, because I'm getting anxious about how long the anxiety will last (and isn't that the kicker?). If I am lucky, my dog Nash will come and lie down with me, letting me pet her with long, gentle strokes that put her to sleep and put me at a little more ease. If I am lucky, the kids will come check on me, just to make sure I'm OK.

And if I'm very lucky, Michael will come in after a while and say the three most romantic words a man can say to his wife after more than two decades of marriage:

"Come, let's walk."

My initial instinct is always to say no. No, I don't want to leave the comfort of my cocoon. No, I don't want to step into the sunshine. No, I don't want to put on a bra.

And then I say yes.

Why? Because going out gives me a change in my physicality, a change in my environment, and a change in my perspective. It reminds me that I have a choice about what I do or don't do, since Michael's invitation is a suggestion, not an obligation. It reminds me that I am strong and able enough to walk unassisted and without pain, which also reminds me to be grateful. It's also proven to have cognitive, physical, and mental health benefits—even in short stints (not sprints).

Even though I have often identified with Woody Allen's quote, "I am at two with nature," I realize that seeing the sky and feeling the fresh air (well, fresh for New York) on my face just feels good. Of course, so does watching Colbert and catching up on business news and celebrity trivia. And that's also the point: I have many good options, and when I'm feeling anxious, I may need to try them all.

Finally, I'm not going it alone. Holding hands with Michael as we take a gentle walk with Nash around the block reminds me that I have people (and other creatures) in my life who care about me, and who want to help me. Talking to Michael about what's weighing on me as we walk is a way to release some of the tension I feel. And being expected to pick up Nash's poop on our walk reminds me that I still have people (and other creatures) who rely on me to take care of them, too.

If today's not a great day for you, put this book down and go outside.

And if today's a great day for you, go outside anyway. We will still be here when you get back. I promise.

SOPHIE'S STRATEGY 31
Call A Professional

In my high school valedictorian speech, I gave my class three pieces of advice:

1. Embrace your flaws.

2. Ask for help.

3. Be curious.

I think that the piece of advice that people need the most is asking for help.

When a lot of us think about asking for help, it scares us. Why do we resist? Because we feel weak and vulnerable.

But the truth is that asking for help is something that strong people do. It's the thing that we do when we realize that we shouldn't have to deal with everything alone. However, even when we feel ready to ask for help, we often don't know where to turn. My suggestion is to call a professional.

A professional doesn't have to be a psychologist or a psychiatrist, although both have been tremendously helpful to me. There are many kinds of professionals who can help people with anxiety. You can also call a fitness trainer. Or a professional organizer. Or a massage therapist.

If you have a problem, I would be willing to bet that there is a professional out there who is trained to help you.

If you are like me, however, you probably think or used to think that you don't need a professional because you can solve your own problems. It's the "I don't need anyone else" mentality. And it is "What do you know about *my* problems?" thinking. But part of calling a professional isn't just getting advice or learning how to do something; it's connecting with other people.

The pure act of reaching out changes everything, even when you don't get the advice or help you need. Reaching out is a step toward acknowledging that you are imperfect, and that is totally OK.

Calling a professional, to me, is like eating crunchy cheese curls. The more you eat, the more you want. And asking for help should be, and I believe is, the same way. The more you ask for help, the more you realize you aren't alone. You start to feel comfortable opening up. And when you do that, you can begin to heal.

DEBORAH'S STRATEGY 32

Do Something Meaningful For Someone Else

"I can barely take care of my own needs—how am I supposed to tend to someone else's?"

"Volunteer? With what extra time?"

"You couldn't pay me enough to volunteer!"

When we're feeling overwhelmed, it can feel like a tough ask to take our limited time, energy, and headspace and give it away. And yet, the benefits of volunteering are tremendous, especially for those of us who struggle with anxiety. It provides engagement, opportunity, learning, impact, connection, perspective, and a distraction from focusing on our own thoughts.

A study by United HealthCare and VolunteerMatch found that volunteering is linked to better physical, mental and emotional health.[20] Here's what folks who volunteered in the last year reported:

- ▶ 25 percent said that volunteering helped them manage a chronic illness.

- ▶ 76 percent said that volunteering made them feel healthier.

- ▶ 78 percent said that volunteering lowers their stress level.

- ▶ 80 percent said that they feel like they have control over their health.

- ▶ 94 percent said that volunteering improved their mood.

---

[20] VolunteerMatch, United HealthCare. "Doing Good Is Good For You," 2017. https://www.unitedhealthgroup.com/content/dam/UHG/PDF/2017/2017_Study-Doing-Good-is-Good-for-You.pdf.

▶ 95 percent said that they are helping to make their community a better place.

▶ 96 percent said that volunteering enriches their sense of purpose in life.

Convinced yet?

Whether you do hands-on volunteering like serving meals at a senior center, or a stretch role like soliciting gifts for your philanthropic organization, or an "I don't want to deal with people" gig like seeding and weeding your community garden, there will be plenty of opportunities for you to do something that matches your interests and the needs of others. (I am hoping that our local hospital needs a volunteer baby cuddler; I would be *brilliant*).

Here are thirty-six other ways that volunteering can reduce your anxiety and increase your sense of peace and purpose:

1. Volunteering can inspire meaningful connections to other people with shared interests, and can combat loneliness, which is a greater health risk than smoking or obesity.

2. Volunteering is correlated to a decreased likelihood of developing high blood pressure (if you're over fifty).

3. Volunteering can help you expand your support system.

4. Volunteering reminds you that you're a part of something bigger than yourself—and bigger than your anxieties.

5. Volunteering can remind you to be grateful for what you have.

6. Volunteering can inspire you to be fully engaged and present, which increases your coping mechanisms, improves your resilience, and boosts your cognitive functioning.

7. Volunteering can inspire you to feel more compassionate toward others.

8. Working with pets and other animals has been shown to improve mood and reduce stress and anxiety.

9. Volunteering increases feelings of self-confidence.

10. Volunteering can help you improve the environment.

11. Volunteering provides a sense of accomplishment.

12. Volunteering offers intellectual and mental stimulation.

13. Volunteering allows you the chance to give back to an organization that you may have been a beneficiary of.

14. Volunteering can offer you a chance to do something aligned with your interests and values (especially if your job or other activities don't).

15. Volunteering can boost your career prospects, especially because recruiters regard volunteerism as an asset.

16. Volunteering can be done in whatever amount of time works for you.

17. Volunteering allows you to dabble in new areas of interest.

18. Volunteering can augment your network.

19. Volunteering can help you learn or master a skill.

20. Volunteering can be done regardless of your level of mobility.

21. Volunteering will give you great stories to share.

22. Volunteering can give you a sense of personal pride.

23. Volunteering allows you to be a voice for those who cannot speak for themselves.

24. Volunteering can offer you travel opportunities.

25. Volunteering lets you recruit like-minded peers and family members to engage with you, thereby multiplying your impact.

26. Volunteering helps you develop leadership skills.

27. Volunteering can allow you to "sample" an industry you might be considering working in one day.

28. Volunteering lets you work alone or with others—and sometimes both.

29. Volunteering makes you a role model for others.

30. Volunteering expands your horizons, exposing you to people, places, and situations you may never have encountered before.

31. Volunteering offers you an insider's perspective on social, political, environmental, health, or other issues.

32. Volunteering can be fun.

33. Volunteering invites you to be creative and innovative.

34. Volunteering allows you to teach others.

35. Volunteering permits you to be as visible or as behind-the-scenes as you'd like.

36. Volunteering sometimes includes free food.

So, what are you ready to sign up for?

SOPHIE'S STRATEGY 33

Use Social Media As Support

One of my favorite things that someone over eighty years old has asked me to do was to "use my Google machine" to find out the definition of *yerd*, which apparently means "to beat someone with a stick."

Now, the point of the previous sentence wasn't to teach you a new word, but to point out that even old people know what Google is, even if they don't know how to use it. I'm not sure if the person who asked me this was mocking my generation, or she really thought that the internet was called the "Google machine". Either way, she really made me think with this comment.

Older people often complain about how much my generation uses the internet. "What's wrong with a book?" "What happened to just calling someone or talking to them in person?"

And they do have a point. When the lady who called the internet the "Google machine" then asked me what the "fuss is" about the internet, I didn't have a good answer.

Much of the stuff on the internet makes people feel bad about themselves. I know personally that I've learned about the dangers of the internet when I allowed it to diagnose my mental illnesses, but there are also many other dangers.

People are constantly comparing themselves to other people on social media. Everyone except you seems "perfect" in their profile picture. We wonder why everyone else seems happy when we are struggling. The internet and social media lead us to this mindset: We aren't good enough, and in order to be happy/successful, we need to follow what other people are doing.

After making the list of all the negative effects of using social media and the "Google machine" I decided to look at it in a different way: What benefits would I be missing if I cut myself off from social media?

When I speak to groups of parents, they often ask me what they should do about their kids using their phones all the time. This is hard for me to answer, because I don't know their kid and everyone is different. But what I always mention is how important it is to *not* cut them off from social media.

A parent's first instinct it to protect their child, and the way they typically want to do that is to shield them from dangers—in this case, what they can find on their phone. Unfortunately, this would mean that those kids wouldn't get the benefits of using social media and the internet to learn about mental health and to find support.

The first Facebook group that I was a part of was a trichotillomania support group. Without that group, I don't know if I ever would have been able to talk about it openly. Knowing that there are more than a thousand people in the group who are not ashamed of their illness was inspiring to me.

I soon joined OCD and panic disorder Facebook groups. Then I followed some mental health Instagram accounts. These are ways to use social media as part of our support system.

To the lady who wondered what the fuss was about the internet and to anyone else who believes, like I did, that social media can only be negative, I challenge you to look at it a different way.

Use the internet and social media to your advantage. Connect with like-minded people. Connect with people who disagree with you and maybe you will learn something. But most importantly, use it to find support, because when all else fails and you don't feel safe talking to someone you know, there is always someone either one mile away or a thousand miles away willing to listen.

DEBORAH'S STRATEGY 34

Make Amends If Your Anxiety Boils Over (And Burns Someone Else)

Author and business leader Margaret Heffernan once remarked, "For good ideas and true innovation, you need human interaction, conflict, argument, debate."

Nevertheless, many of us would rather not engage in conflict, argument or debate (and maybe even avoid human interaction altogether). We work hard to minimize interpersonal tension and stay quiet in the face of differences of opinion or perspective—especially if disagreeing (or being seen as disagreeable) makes you feel anxious.

Here's the problem: if you're the kind of person who would rather keep your difference of perspective to yourself, your constant attempts to keep your opinions—and your anxiety—under control can backfire.

According to research published in the journal *Social Psychological and Personality Science*, bottling up your emotions can ultimately make you more aggressive.[21] When we can't or don't express our emotions, like feeling anxious, disappointed, or even helpless, we are more likely to act out after.

So, what does that look like? It can look like you're going from placid and serene to explosive and combative in the blink of an eye. This can quickly undermine the trust you've built with others, and make you seem unpredictable and erratic. If and when that happens, you have some personal work to do, so that you can identify, manage and express your emotions in a healthier way next time. You also have some relationship repair to engage in if you want to prevent a similar scenario from repeating itself.

---

[21] Bushman, Brad J, "Does Venting Anger Feed or Extinguish the Flame? Catharsis, Rumination, Distraction, Anger, and Aggressive Responding" SAGE Journals, June 1, 2002. https://journals.sagepub.com/doi/abs/10.1177/0146167202289002.

Here are three things to do if and when your anxiety boils over—
and burns someone else:

Make a reparation. Offer a genuine apology for your tone
of voice and the content of your message, especially if it
may be perceived as aggressive, rude, defensive, critical or
condescending. "I'm sorry for what I said and for how I said
it. I felt angry and I didn't control my temper," is a simple
version. Other language with which you take full responsibility
and communicate your regret works, too. Keep in mind that
an apology shouldn't be any version of "I'm sorry that you..."
("are an idiot," "don't understand simple logic," "made me
lose my temper," etc.) Blaming the other person for your
(momentary) inability to behave respectfully is a disrespectful and
counterproductive move.

Express appreciation. Chances are, there's something to be
grateful for, even when you're feeling bad about what happened.
You might say, "Thank you for staying and listening to me, even
when I raised my voice." Or, "While I don't like how I spoke
to you, I am grateful that you were willing to explain your
perspective to me." Or, "Thank you for helping us have the
conversation we needed to have, even if I didn't behave the way
I'd wanted to." Or even, "Thank you for recognizing that I wasn't
at my best, and for suggesting we take a break and regroup." A
little gratitude will go a long way.

Offer an invitation. Just because the argument might be over,
that doesn't mean the relationship will immediately bounce back.
And just because you may have moved past it, that doesn't mean
the other person has. Offer a genuine invitation to continue the
discussion and hear their perspective—whether it's about the
content or the impact that your behavior had. You could start by
telling the other person how much you value your relationship,
and then ask, "What do you want me to know about how you're
feeling?" You might offer, "What do I need to clean up with you
in order for us to move forward?" And you could say, "You might
not be ready to talk about what happened now, but I'm always
open to discussing it with you. Would you please come talk to me
when you're ready?"

In the words of author David Augsburger, "The more we run from conflict, the more it masters us; the more we try to avoid it, the more it controls us; the less we fear conflict, the less it confuses us; the less we deny our differences, the less they divide us."

SOPHIE'S STRATEGY 35

When Connecting With A Companion, Think Broadly

The first thing I think of when I hear the phrase "connect with others" is connecting with *people*. Now, if you are like me at all, this may intimidate you. I mean, talking to other people can be scary. But what I've found is that when I feel anxious, connecting with an animal makes me feel better.

Almost two years ago, after dealing with months of horrible and debilitating panic attacks, my family and I rescued our dog, Nash. To many people, this came as a huge surprise, because since my mom was little, she has always been terrified of dogs. Nevertheless, we made a place in our home and our hearts for an eighty-pound pit bull who had been abused and abandoned and who, like me, was ready to start a happier life.

When she first came home, she was nervous, hiding under tables and shaking in the dark. But anxiety was something I knew how to deal with. I promised her I wouldn't let her sleep alone until she was ready. Every night, I sang to her until she fell asleep. Every day, I took her on long walks, always returning us back to her new, loving home.

She quickly returned the favor. During my panic attacks, I called for her, and she licked my face until I stopped crying (she couldn't sing, so this worked). When I felt numb to the world, she was there, demanding to be stroked and helping me ground myself in something real. And when I came home from school overwhelmed, she desperately needed to pee. That helped me reorder my priorities. I didn't have the option to panic.

Animals, and dogs in particular, have a unique way of improving our mental health. They force us to go outside and get fresh air. They have needs which we need to take care of, shifting the focus from ourselves, where anxiety starts, to someone else. Caring for another living creature also gives people a sense of purpose, which is something those with mental illnesses often lack.

According to a recent compilation of evidence published online:

▶ Pet owners are less likely to suffer from depression than those without pets.

▶ People with pets have lower blood pressure in stressful situations than those without pets. One study even found that when people with borderline hypertension adopted dogs from a shelter, their blood pressure declined significantly within five months.

▶ Playing with a dog or cat can elevate levels of serotonin and dopamine, which calm and relax.

▶ Pet owners have lower triglyceride and cholesterol levels (indicators of heart disease) than those without pets.

▶ Heart attack patients with pets survive longer than those without.

▶ Pet owners over age 65 make 30 percent fewer visits to their doctors than those without pets.[22]

Animals are amazing creatures. For me, getting Nash saved my life. And I mean it. So, when we think about connecting with others, think broadly. Don't just think people. Know that your options of who to connect with are unlimited.

---

[22] "Mood-Boosting Power of Pets," HelpGuide.org, June 24, 2019, https://www.help-guide.org/articles/mental-health/mood-boosting-power-of-dogs.htm.

DEBORAH'S STRATEGY 36
Say No *If That's The Right Choice For Now*

You have to decide what your highest priorities are and have the courage pleasantly, smilingly, and unapologetically—to say no to other things. And the way to do that is by having a bigger yes burning inside.

—Stephen Covey

When you're feeling anxious, you may have no idea what you're saying *yes* to—especially if your head is flooded with doubts, fears, insecurities, and lots of other voices you're trying to say *no* to. Like what? Like "No, I'm not a fraud" or "No, I won't fail that test" or "No, I won't bomb that presentation."

Trying to say *no* to all of those inner voices can be exhausting. What makes it even more stressful is then trying to figure out how to thoughtfully, assertively, and respectfully say *no* to anyone or anything else that will add more strife and struggle for you right now.

I say "right now" because isolating yourself isn't a smart, healthy, or sustainable option over the long term, which is why this section is called "Connect with Others." Nevertheless, choosing to say *no* on occasion can be a *yes* to yourself—to your emotional, intellectual, spiritual, and physical well-being.

And yes, you can say *no* to a request, because a request is not a command. A request is an ask, to which we can say *yes, no,* or make a counteroffer. A command assumes an obligation. However, we often think of requests as commands, sometimes due to the tone in which the request is made, or a power differential, or our fear of the other person's reaction, or even a feeling of indebtedness.

While we all know that "No" is a complete sentence when it comes to responding to a request, we often wrestle with being too passive (when we want to avoid conflict or hurt feelings), too aggressive (when we worry our needs will be ignored), or even too passive-aggressive (when we're feeling manipulated, punished, or otherwise concerned that an honest or direct approach won't work).

A passive approach to saying *no* might sound like "OK, I'll do it... *this* time," when we don't want to do it this time (or at all). Or it could sound like, "Maybe I can," when you already know that you can't or don't want to say *yes*.

An aggressive reaction to a request for our time might range from asking, "Are you stupid? I said no!" to, "Not in a million years," or even, "What makes you think I would want to do that?"

A passive-aggressive response can sound like, "Fine" (when you're anything but). It can also sound like, "Do I really have a choice?" It also shows up as, "I'll get back to you," (and you don't) or, "Yeah, sure, I'll be there" (and then you "forget" to show up).

As much as we don't want to disappoint, hurt, or even anger friends, colleagues, and family members, we can be assertive and firm in our *nos* while being flexible enough to keep the door open for future *yeses*. This requires us to be clear and honest about our own needs and preferences (to do something else with our time and energy, especially when we're struggling) while honoring the needs and preferences of others (to be heard, to feel appreciated, to stay connected, to avoid embarrassment, to maintain their dignity in the face of rejection, etc.).

Here are ten ways to say no assertively to a request for your time:

1. That sounds like a fantastic event/opportunity/cause, and I know that I will be sorry to miss it.

2. Normally, I would say yes, but I have already committed to _____. [Note: "I have already committed to taking some time for myself" is a reasonable response].

3. Right now, I am saying no to all invitations (on this topic, at this time frame, etc.). Here's why. [Feel free to share as much or as little as you feel comfortable.]

4. I need to decline, but I do hope you'll keep me in mind for the future. Would you please reach out again?

5. Not this time, but I am so flattered you thought of me for this.

6. I sit down with my calendar on Sundays. Would you please send me all of the information I need, and I'll let you know on Monday if it works with my whole schedule?

7. I can't make a decision right now, and I don't want to hold you up so feel free to ask someone else.

8. Not this time, but when's the next opportunity available for something like this?

9. When do you need to know by? I ask because if it's in the next [week/month/quarter], I will need to say no.

10. I'm not available, but I know someone who would love to be a part of it. May I connect you?

And just for fun, here's how *not* to say *no*:

▶ You're joking, right?

▶ This request is below my pay grade.

▶ I wish I had the luxury of entertaining such a whimsical request.

▶ You're into that kind of thing?

▶ Sure, at half-past never.

▶ Yuck!

▶ *N* to the *O*.

It turns out there's no prize for being she who suffers secretly in silence, unless you consider loneliness a reward. If you're not OK, you might as well not pretend you are, especially since life has a way of holding us down until we utter that magic word, HELP! That's when angels rush to your side.
—Glennon Doyle

EPILOGUE

Overcoming Overthinking And Beyond

Anxiety can be a monster. Anyone who has lived with it knows the sensation of being overwhelmed, feeling helpless—and wondering if it's hopeless.

It isn't hopeless. And you aren't helpless.

Both of us are proof that you can live a happy and successful life with everyday anxiety or even chronic anxiety. Both of us know how much of a burden anxiety can be, and we also know how to turn it into one of your greatest assets. And, both of us know that once you help yourself, you can start to help others, too.

That's why we wrote this book. These thirty-six strategies are a place to start to help you overcome your overthinking—and the starting spot for you to share what worked for you with others who struggle, too.

Whether you found a dozen tips that really resonate, or one or two that you turn into daily practices, know that doing *something* is already a powerful, positive, healthy choice for yourself.

We won't tell you to "just relax" or "get over it."

We won't tell you that you've got nothing to worry about.

We *will* tell you that you're not alone, and that we're here for you—just like we are, and have always been, for each other.

Wondering if you should reach out to us? Don't overthink it! Just do it:

Authors@OvercomingOverthinking.com

With our support,
Deborah and Sophie

Acknowledgments

This book would not have been possible without the support of our family. Michael and Jake, you both have been unconditionally loving toward both of us. We appreciate your learning about our experiences and understanding the ways in which you are able to make us less anxious.

We would also like to thank everyone out there who has been following both of us in our emotional journey to overcome mental illness and who have been brave enough to take steps to help themselves too.

To our wonderful publishers at Indie Books International, we are grateful for your commitment to helping our vision become a reality.

Thank you to all of our readers for taking the time to take care of yourselves.

About The Authors

Deborah Grayson Riegel is an executive coach, speaker, and author focused on helping professionals become more confident and persuasive presenters, communicators, and leaders. She has taught management communication at Wharton Business School and executive communications at the Beijing International MBA Program at Peking University, China. Deborah holds a BA in psychology from The University of Michigan, a Masters of Social Work from Columbia University, and is a certified coach with the International Coach Federation. Deborah writes for *Harvard Business Review, Inc., Forbes, Fast Company, Psychology Today,* and other publications. She lives with her husband Michael and rescue dog, Nash, who loves her best. When she isn't speaking, coaching, or writing, she can be found in the throw pillow section of HomeGoods. You can visit her online at www.gettalksupport.com.

Sophie Riegel is a two-time published author, a professional speaker, and a mental health advocate. Sophie began speaking across the country to share her experience with mental illness with both teens and adults after publishing her first book at age seventeen: *Don't Tell Me To Relax: One Teen's Journey to Survive Anxiety (and How You Can, Too).* She also works hard to help others understand the true impact of mental illness and the importance of talking openly about mental health. Sophie has articles published on *Thrive Global, My Jewish Learning, The Nassau Herald,* and has recorded multiple podcasts, all available for free on her website: donttellmetorelaxbook.com. Her message has reached thousands of people and she hopes to expand her project even more. Sophie is a full-time student at Duke University and plans on writing her third book in the near future.

Works Referenced

"About Betty Alice Erickson." Ericksonian Info. Accessed August 29, 2019. http://ericksonian.info/author/betty/.

Anxiety and Depression Association of America (ADAA), Facts and Statistics page. Accessed August 29, 2019. https://adaa.org/about-adaa/press-room/facts-statistics.

Ashforth, Blake E. *Role Transitions in Organizational Life: an Identity-Based Perspective.* New York, NY: Routledge, 2012.

Bodnarchuk, Kari. "Preparing Kids for When a Parent Travels." *The Boston Globe*, BostonGlobe.com, June 6, 2015. https://www.bostonglobe.com/lifestyle/travel/2015/06/06/preparing-kids-for-when-parent-travels/ud1ZhHggFGhwvEZ54IUDUN/story.html.

Bushman, Brad J, "Does Venting Anger Feed or Extinguish the Flame? Catharsis, Rumination, Distraction, Anger, and Aggressive Responding" SAGE Journals, June 1, 2002. https://journals.sagepub.com/doi/abs/10.1177/0146167202289002.

Burton, Robert. "Where Science and Story Meet - Preview Issue: The Story of Nautilus." Nautilus, April 22, 2013. http://nautil.us/issue/0/the-story-of-nautilus/where-science-and-story-meet.

"Disclosing to Others," NAMI, Accessed August 29, 2019. https://www.nami.org/find-support/living-with-a-mental-health-condition/disclosing-to-others.

Eurich, Tasha. *Insight: the Surprising Truth about How Others See Us, How We See Ourselves, and Why the Answers Matter More than We Think.* New York: Currency, 2018.

Foer, Jonathan Safran. *Extremely Loud & Incredibly Close.* London: Penguin Books, 2018.

Formica, Michael J. "Self-Blame: The Ultimate Emotional Abuse." Psychology Today. Sussex Publishers, April 19, 2013. https://www.psychologytoday.com/us/blog/enlightened-living/201304/self-blame-the-ultimate-emotional-abuse.

Gottman.com, The Gottman Institute.

Grant, Adam. "WorkLife with Adam Grant: Bouncing Back from Rejection on Apple Podcasts." Apple Podcasts, April 16, 2019. https://podcasts.apple.com/us/podcast/bouncing-back-from-rejection/id1346314086?i=1000435037507.

Heath, Chip, and Dan Heath. *Switch: How to Change Things When Change Is Hard*. Erscheinungsort nicht ermittelbar: Random House US, 2013.

Hibbert, Christina. "Exercise For Mental Health: 8 Keys To Get And Stay Moving." NAMI, May 23, 2016. https://www.nami.org/blogs/nami-blog/may-2016/exercise-for-mental-health-8-keys-to-get-and-stay.

Jeffrey, Scott. "9 Grounding Techniques to Reduce Anxiety and Center Yourself." Scott Jeffrey, August 14, 2019. https://scottjeffrey.com/grounding-techniques/.

Karpman, Stephen B. "Listening, Learning, and Accountability: Three Rules of Openness, Three Rules of Accountability, and the Adult Scales, Listening Scales, and Listener's Loops." Semantic Scholar, January 1, 1970. https://www.semanticscholar.org/paper/Listening%2C-Learning%2C-and-Accountability%3A-Three-of-Karpman/e07b5fb75e76bc0cf646b800893fe79fc570ba81.

"Mood-Boosting Power of Pets." HelpGuide.org, June 24, 2019. https://www.helpguide.org/articles/mental-health/mood-boosting-power-of-dogs.htm.

Neff, Kristin. "Self-Compassion: An Alternative Conceptualization of a HealthyAttitudeToward Oneself." *Psychology Press*, Taylor & Francis Group, 2003.

Trzeciak, Stephen, and Anthony Mazzarelli. *Compassionomics: the Revolutionary Scientific Evidence That Caring Makes a Difference*. Pensacola: Studer Group, 2019.

Turkle, Sherry. "Stop Googling. Let's Talk." *The New York Times*, September 26, 2015. https://www.nytimes.com/2015/09/27/opinion/sunday/stop-googling-lets-talk.html.

VolunteerMatch, United HealthCare. "Doing Good Is Good For You," 2017. https://www.unitedhealthgroup.com/content/dam/UHG/PDF/2017/2017_Study-Doing-Good-is-Good-for-You.pdf.